ENGLISH MORPHOLC ___
LANGUAGE TEACHING PROFESSION

This highly accessible book presents an overview of English morphology for all those involved in the English-language teaching industry. For non-native learners, the ability to recognize and produce new words in appropriate circumstances is a challenging task, and knowledge of the word-building system of English is essential to effective language learning. This book clearly explains the morphology of English from the point of view of the non-native learner and shows how teachers and professors can instruct EFL students successfully with effective materials.

Covering the scope of the task of teaching English morphology specifically to non-native learners of English, bestselling authors Bauer and Nation provide a range of strategies and tactics for straightforward instruction, and demonstrate how teachers of English as a foreign language can easily integrate learning of the morphological system into their language courses. This book helps teachers and learners make sensible decisions about where to focus deliberate attention, what to be careful about, and what not to be concerned about. It offers a range of shortcuts, tips and tricks for teaching, and gives detailed practical information on topics including:

* Sound and spelling
* Possessives
* Comparative and superlative
* Past tense and past participle
* Making nouns, verbs, adjectives, adverbs and words with prefixes
* Learned word-formation.

This book is essential and practical reading for graduate students on English-language teaching courses, preservice teachers, consultants, practitioners, researchers and scholars in ELT.

Laurie Bauer is Emeritus Professor of Linguistics at Victoria University of Wellington, New Zealand.

I.S.P. Nation is Emeritus Professor of Applied Linguistics at Victoria University of Wellington, New Zealand.

ESL & APPLIED LINGUISTICS PROFESSIONAL SERIES

Eli Hinkel, Series Editor

Teaching Academic L2 Writing
Practical Techniques in Vocabulary and Grammar
Eli Hinkel

Quality in TESOL and Teacher Education
From a Results Culture Towards a Quality Culture
Juan de Dios Martínez Agudo

Language Curriculum Design, 2nd Edition
John Macalister, I.S.P. Nation

Teaching Extensive Reading in Another Language
I.S.P. Nation, Rob Waring

English Language Proficiency Testing in Asia
A New Paradigm Bridging Global and Local Contexts
Edited by Lily I-Wen Su, Cyril J. Weir, Jessica R. W. Wu

English Morphology for the Language Teaching Profession
Laurie Bauer with I.S.P. Nation

For more information about this series, please visit: www.routledge.com/ESL-Applied-Linguistics-Professional-Series/book-series/LEAESLALP

ENGLISH MORPHOLOGY FOR THE LANGUAGE TEACHING PROFESSION

Laurie Bauer with I.S.P. Nation

Routledge
Taylor & Francis Group

NEW YORK AND LONDON

First published 2020
by Routledge
52 Vanderbilt Avenue, New York, NY 10017

and by Routledge
2 Park Square, Milton Park, Abingdon, Oxon, OX14 4RN

Routledge is an imprint of the Taylor & Francis Group, an informa business

© 2020 Taylor & Francis

Library of Congress Cataloging-in-Publication Data
Names: Bauer, Laurie, 1949– author. | Nation, I.S.P., author.
Title: English morphology for the language teaching profession /
Laurie Bauer with I.S.P. Nation.
Description: New York: Routledge, 2020. |
Includes bibliographical references and index. |
Identifiers: LCCN 2019049112 (print) | LCCN 2019049113 (ebook) |
ISBN 9780367428020 (hardback) | ISBN 9780367428013 (paperback) |
ISBN 9780367855222 (ebook)
Subjects: LCSH: English language–Morphology. |
English language–Word formation. Classification: LCC PE1171 .B38 2020 (print) |
LCC PE1171 (ebook) | DDC 425/.9–dc23
LC record available at https://lccn.loc.gov/2019049112
LC ebook record available at https://lccn.loc.gov/2019049113

ISBN: 978-0-367-42802-0 (hbk)
ISBN: 978-0-367-42801-3 (pbk)
ISBN: 978-0-367-85522-2 (ebk)

Typeset in Bembo
by Newgen Publishing UK

CONTENTS

TABLES

NOTATIONAL CONVENTIONS

★	what follows is not good English
Italics	used to mark example words or longer stretches of language used as examples
Br	more usual in British English (see p. 20)
US	more usual in American English (see p. 20)
CL	consonant letter
Cs	consonant sound
VL	vowel letter
Vs	vowel sound
<...>	enclose spellings
[...]	enclose representations of sounds
~	alternates with, is found in variation with; [in statements of meaning] the meaning of the base
>	gives rise to the next form
<	arises from the next form
esp.	especially
N, V, Adj, Adv	noun, verb, adjective, adverb
-al]N	The suffix *-al* which creates nouns (and so on)
SG, PL	singular, plural

For transcription symbols, see pp. 22–3.

PREFACE

This book presents an overview of English morphology for those involved in the English-language teaching industry. It is not an introductory text, but can be used by advanced students, as well as by teachers, textbook writers, curriculum designers, and anyone else interested in the minutiae of the word-structure of English. At the same time, it is not exhaustive. There are many affixes, or potential affixes, which it does not deal with – sometimes because they are too rare, sometimes because they are too restricted in their domain, sometimes because they are no longer perceived as affixes by native speakers of English. Also, the huge topic of compounding is given relatively little coverage, only the most productive patterns being discussed in any detail. This is not only because what counts as a compound in English is controversial (which it is), but also because the full coverage would demand so much detail that it would not be useful in the language-teaching situation.

We should like to thank Stuart McLean, Liza Tarasova and referees for Routledge for their comments on earlier drafts of this work.

1

LEARNING ENGLISH MORPHOLOGY

Native-speaking children learn new words at an amazing rate of around 1,000 word families a year. For non-native learners, being able to recognize and produce new words in appropriate circumstances is a much more challenging task. As with native speakers, non-native learners could use a number of strategies, from guesswork to overt requests for explanation. All such strategies are valuable. In this book we consider only one of these strategies, but one which has the potential to provide a large amount of support, and only for one language, namely exploitation of the morphological system of English. This means that we can provide no support in learning words such as *dog, oak, elephant, satellite* and *tomato*. These have to be guessed from context, recognized because of similarity to equivalent words in other familiar languages, or studied, or picked up by frequent exposure. But huge numbers of the words of English are not totally arbitrary, as these are. They are partly motivated, in that their structure reflects something of their meaning, and systematic exploitation of this motivation can ease the load of learning new vocabulary items. Some of the words whose structure leads to helpful clues are words which native speaking children acquire in the first few years of life. Some are words which native speakers learn only when they get to secondary or tertiary education. The basic principles of morphological analysis are thus not principles which are useful only at one stage of language learning, nor are they principles which we can discard after we have used them to set up a few basic patterns. They are fundamental to the learning of new vocabulary throughout the learning experience, and need to be continually modified to take account of structures which have become newly relevant. That is what makes morphology, and morphological analysis, a tool of ongoing importance in language learning, even if it is not the only tool for learning new vocabulary.

1.1 Word Building

Young native speakers learn much of the morphological system of English largely without any direct instruction, and young learners of English as a second language who live and participate in the culture of an English-speaking country learn in much the same way. Learners of English as a foreign language however face a much more difficult learning task. The aim of this book is to show the scope of this task, to suggest a range of possible shortcuts, and to show teachers of English as a foreign language how to integrate learning of the morphological system into their language course.

1.2 The Scope of the Task

Every English sentence involves some use of the English morphological system, and one of the very important ways in which a learner's vocabulary grows is through adding more members to existing word families. A word family consists of a base form (sometimes called a stem form) and its closely related inflected and derived forms which all build on the same core meaning of the base form. There are different levels of word families depending on the various prefixes and suffixes which are considered to be within the knowledge of language learners at certain proficiency levels. There is considerable debate about what level of word family best describes the proficiency level of various learners of English as a foreign language from different language backgrounds. This is because the definition of a word family needs to change as learners' knowledge of the morphological system of English develops.

Bauer and Nation (1993), largely with learners of English as a foreign language in mind, set up a system of seven word family levels of cumulatively increasing size. The first six levels range from the most basic level, Level 1, where every word form is considered a different word, to Level 6 which includes all the inflections and a large number of derivational affixes which can be added to free bases. Level 7 includes classical roots and affixes which involve bound bases. Table 1.1 from Bauer and Nation shows these seven levels.

The levels are cumulative so that, for example, Level 3 includes not only the affixes introduced at Level 3 but also the inflections at Level 2. The levels are based on the criteria of frequency, regularity, productivity and predictability, so, for example, the affixes introduced at Level 4 are generally more frequent, regular, productive and predictable than those introduced at Level 5.

Table 1.2 contains some examples of different levels of word families based on the word bases *teach* (a verb) and *eye* (a noun).

At Level 2, the definition of a word family could require the base form and all the family members to be the same part of speech. This definition distinguishing parts of speech is called a *lemma*. A more inclusive definition at Level 2 would allow different parts of speech to be members of the same word family. So *eye* as a

TABLE 1.1 A summary of Bauer and Nation's (1993) seven word family levels

Level 1

A different form is a different word. Capitalization is ignored.

Level 2

Regularly inflected words are part of the same family. The inflectional categories are – plural; third person singular present tense; past tense; past participle; -*ing*; comparative; superlative; possessive.

Level 3

-able, -er, -ish, -less, -ly, -ness, -th, -y, non-, un-, all with restricted uses.

Level 4

-al, -ation, -ess, -ful, -ism, -ist, -ity, -ize, -ment, -ous, in-, all with restricted uses.

Level 5

-age (leakage), -al (arrival), -ally (idiotically), -an (American), -ance (clearance), -ant (consultant), -ary (revolutionary), -atory (confirmatory), -dom (kingdom; officialdom), -eer (black marketeer), -en (wooden), -en (widen), -ence (emergence), -ent (absorbent), -ery (bakery; trickery), -ese (Japanese; officialese), -esque (picturesque), -ette (usherette; roomette), -hood (childhood), -i (Israeli), -ian (phonetician; Johnsonian), -ite (Paisleyite; also chemical meaning), -let (coverlet), -ling (duckling), -ly (leisurely), -most (topmost), -ory (contradictory), -ship (studentship), -ward (homeward), -ways (crossways), -wise (endwise; discussion-wise), anti- (anti-inflation), ante- (anteroom), arch- (archbishop), bi- (biplane), circum- (circumnavigate), counter- (counter-attack), en- (encage; enslave), ex- (ex-president), fore- (forename), hyper- (hyperactive), inter- (inter-African, interweave), mid- (mid-week), mis- (misfit), neo- (neo-colonialism), post- (post-date), pro- (pro-British), semi- (semi-automatic), sub- (subclassify; subterranean), un- (untie; unburden).

Level 6

-able, -ee, -ic, -ify, -ion, -ist, -ition, -ive, -th, -y, pre-, re-.

Level 7

Classical roots and affixes.

noun and *eye* as a verb could be counted in the same word family at Level 2 using the more inclusive definition. This type of family unit at Level 2 has been called a *flemma* following Pinchbeck (see Nation 2016: 26). In Table 1.2 we have used the narrower definition, *teaching* as a verb is listed separately from *teaching* as a noun. From Level 3 on, family members do not need to be the same part of speech. At Level 6 the related forms of *teach* make one family, but at Level 2 at the level of the lemma, the same forms make seven different families.

The idea behind the word family is that a family member should require no or little additional learning for it to be recognized as a member of the family, as

TABLE 1.2 Examples of word families at different family levels

Level 2 families	Level 3 families	Level 6 family
teach	teach	teach
taught	taught	taught
teaches	untaught	untaught
teaching	teacher	teachable
teaching	teacherly	unteachable
teachings	teachers	teacher
teacher	teaches	teacherly
teachers	teaching	teachers
teacherly	teachings	teaches
untaught	teachable	teaching
teachable	unteachable	teachings
unteachable		
eye	eye	eye
eyes	eyes	eyes
eye	eyed	eyed
eyes	eyeing	eyeful
eyed	eying	eyefuls
eyeing	eyeful	eyeing
eying	eyefuls	eying
eyeful	eyeless	eyeless
eyefuls	eyelet	eyelet
eyeless	eyelets	eyelets
eyelet		
eyelets		

long as the base or some of the other family members are known, and as long as the learner is familiar with the form and meaning of the prefixes and suffixes that are part of the particular family member. It should be obvious from this definition that what is seen as a family member depends on the learners' knowledge of the morphological system.

The most useful way to decide what words to present in an English course involves dividing the words into levels based on their range and frequency of occurrence. Typically this has been done by organizing words into groups or levels of 1,000 word families. The most frequent 1,000 words cover around 85% of the running words in a text (Webb & Nation 2017), the second most frequent 1,000 around 5%, and so on with a smaller coverage for each successive 1,000 words. A set of frequency-based word lists called the BNC/COCA lists can be found on I.S.P Nation's website: www.victoria.ac.nz/lals/staff/paul-nation.aspx.

Most English words can be seen as part of word families. A few high frequency families have only one member, for example *the, beneath* and *also*. Some have a very large number of members which include both British and American spellings, for example, *centre* with at least thirty members. High frequency words tend to have larger families than low frequency words. If we take Level 6 of Bauer and Nation as our criterion for family membership, the words in the first and second 1,000 average around 6 or 7 words per family (for example: *answer, answerable, answered, answering, answers, unanswerable, unanswered*) and there is a steady reduction in word family size, with the tenth 1,000 words having a family size just under 3 members per family (*abject, abjectly, abjectness*), and the twentieth 1,000 having a family size under 2 members per family (*ammonoid, ammonoids*).

1.3 The Importance of Morphological Knowledge

There are several reasons why a learner of English as a foreign language needs to become familiar with the word-building system of English.

1. Frequency: Almost every English sentence requires a language user to make some kind of interpretation or decision involving the inflectional suffixes of English, and most word families involve inflectional and derivational affixes. In a typical English text, over one-fifth of the running words are inflected and one-eighth of the running words have a derivational affix (Nagy & Anderson 1984).

2. Meaningfulness: Prefixes and suffixes affect the meanings of words. This is most obvious with derivational affixes, because most derivational suffixes signal the part of speech of a word and many prefixes and suffixes add some additional meaning. While inflectional suffixes do not change the part of speech, they indicate tense, number, possession and degree. Parts of words add to the meaning of the words containing them.

3. Correctness: Lack of use of affixes and misuse of affixes affect the correctness of speech and writing. Learning the inflectional suffixes of English can be a major challenge, even for learners whose first language contains similar features. For learners whose first language does not contain such features, gaining control of some of the inflectional suffixes requires major conceptual change. For nouns, this requires developing concepts of countable and uncountable, and singular and plural. For verbs, this requires developing concepts of person, past and present, active and passive, perfect, and progressive. Because most derivational suffixes affect the part of speech, the use of the appropriate derived form involves decisions relating to grammar.

4. Vocabulary growth: Our vocabulary size increases when we learn new words. It also increases when we learn the derived forms of base words we already know. Anglin (1993) used the term 'morphological problem-solving' to describe the use of affix knowledge to understand the meaning of words. A word with an affix, such as *slowness*, may be related to a word we already know, *slow*. However, *slowness* is still a new word to learn. If we already know slow and have some experience with -*ness* in other words, then understanding and learning *slowness* is initially a much easier task than learning a completely new word.

5. Repetition: Repetition is the major factor affecting vocabulary learning. If we want to learn something, we need to meet it several times at spaced intervals with the opportunity to recall knowledge gained from previous meetings. There are two kinds of repetition – verbatim repetition where we meet the same item again, and varied repetition where we meet an item again but in different circumstances. When we meet the inflected or derived form of a word base we have met before, this meeting can be a repetition if we can see the connection between the base and the affixed form. If we cannot see the connection, then meeting the affixed form is like meeting a new unknown word. The average word family at Level 6 of Bauer and Nation (1993) contains a base form, around two to four inflected forms depending on part of speech, and somewhere between two and four derived forms (Nagy & Anderson 1984), for example, *agree, agreeable, agreeably, agreed, agreeing, agreement, agreements*. If learners have the skill and knowledge to recognize word parts and relate them to the meaning of words, they greatly increase the number of repetitions of the words they need to learn. Instead of just experiencing a repetition when exactly the same form is met (a verbatim repetition), they can experience a repetition when the same form or a related form is met (a varied repetition). So, when a learner meets *agree* or *agreement* or *agreed*, each meeting can be seen as a repetition of the same family. This makes a large increase in the opportunities for repetition. On average for the higher frequency words, it increases the opportunities for repetition around four or five times. Even with low frequency words, being able to recognize related forms doubles or triples the opportunities for repetition.

6. Learning strategies: Learning strategies typically involve the conscious application of procedures to help learning. Vocabulary learning strategies include guessing from context, using word-cards or electronic flash-cards, using memory tricks such as the keyword technique, and dictionary use. There is also a word part strategy that can be used to help words stay in memory (Nation 2013a: chapter 9). This strategy involves breaking a word into parts and then relating the meaning of the parts to the meaning of the word. For example, if we meet the word *prefix*, we can break the word into the parts *pre* and *fix*, and if we know the meaning of *pre* meaning 'before', we can relate this meaning to the meaning of the whole word. This is a kind of memory trick, using analysis, to help the newly met word stick in memory by relating the new knowledge (the form and meaning of the word) to familiar knowledge (the meaning of the parts) (Wei 2015). To apply the word part strategy, a learner needs to be familiar with the most useful word parts (particularly prefixes), and needs to be able to break words into parts.

7. Quality of processing: Analysing words adds to the depth of mental processing of those words and thus helps them stick in memory. In this way gaining and using morphological knowledge is a kind of mnemonic to support vocabulary learning, even if it is not used systematically as a learning strategy.

Varied repetition

Nau 2015

There is plenty of evidence that some learners of English as a foreign language have very poor control of English morphology, and that their morphological knowledge is not keeping pace with their vocabulary knowledge (McLean 2018; Mochizuki & Aizawa 2000; Ward & Chuenjundaeng 2009). What should be clear from this brief survey is that there are strong arguments for helping learners develop knowledge of word parts.

1.4 What Learners Need to Know ⟶ Important argument former

Learners need to develop a range of knowledge involving word parts. They need to develop the meta-linguistic knowledge that English makes use of word parts and that these parts contribute to the meaning and use of the words containing them. They also need to know that being aware of these word parts can contribute to the learning and understanding of words. More particularly, they need to know the forms and meanings of the most common word parts, and should be able to recognize them when they occur in words. With the help of context clues if necessary, they need to be able to interpret the meaning of words containing known parts. This recognition and interpretation of word parts needs to be strategic so that learners have the best possible chance of making a correct interpretation. Learners also need to develop systematic productive knowledge of word parts. Learners also need to know how to use word parts as a mnemonic support for helping words stick in memory. In the next section we look at a wide range of complementary ways for developing this knowledge.

1.5 How to Develop Morphological Knowledge

When considering how to develop any aspect of language knowledge or language use, it is helpful to draw on a broad framework such as the four strands to ensure that all options are considered

The principle of the four strands can be used to guide curriculum design. It states that a well-balanced language course should have four equal strands of meaning-focused input, meaning-focused output, language-focused learning and fluency development (Nation 2007, 2013b). This is another way of saying that language learning should occur through a balanced mixture of learning through use and learning through deliberate attention to language features. Ideally, the ideas content and language content of these strands should be integrated so that there are maximal opportunities for repetition of vocabulary.

The four strands can be applied to any particular aspect of language learning such as reading, grammar, or morphology. When asking a question such as how do you teach reading? how is grammar learned?, the question can be usefully rephrased as how does learning to read a foreign language fit into the four strands? or how should we expect grammar to be learned across the four strands?

How can knowledge of morphology develop across the four strands? We can expect knowledge of word parts to develop incidentally through reading and listening (meaning-focused input). The more learners read and listen to the language at levels that are appropriate to their current proficiency level, the more they meet words containing affixes that they need to comprehend. Meaning-focused input at the right level sets up the learning conditions of repetition, spaced retrieval and varied meetings in meaningful contexts, and we can expect reasonable amounts of morphological knowledge to develop through guessing from context while listening and reading. A teacher needs to ensure that learners are doing plenty of extensive listening and extensive reading. Extensive reading is such a valuable source of input for language learning that the teacher needs to make sure that learners do the reading by setting monitored course requirements, that learners get hooked on reading by making sure that many interesting books at the right level are available, and that the reading is put to use through related activities such as book discussion groups. Learners may interrupt their reading to apply word part analysis strategies or to draw on first language knowledge of cognates in order to do morphological problem-solving in the context of reading. While this interruption is most properly classified as language-focused learning, it springs from dealing with language in use.

Meaning-focused output encourages the productive use of knowledge of word parts. This learning through speaking and writing is reliant on knowledge gained from meaning-focused input and language-focused learning. It provides the opportunity to use productively what has been learned and to experiment using known rules. A teacher needs to ensure that learners are doing plenty of meaning-focused speaking interacting with others, and are doing plenty of writing with a real communicative purpose (see Nation 2013b for ways of doing this). This interaction will provide opportunities to apply known morphological rules and will encourage the creative use of what is known.

Language-focused learning involves deliberate attention to language features. Language-focused learning can occur when teachers teach and when learners study, and when learners receive feedback. Language-focused learning also includes strategy training, and the strategies of guessing from context, word-cards, word parts and dictionary use are all relevant to the development of morphological knowledge. In a later part of this chapter we will look closely at how language-focused learning applies to word part learning and the various activities involving word parts.

The fourth strand is the strand of fluency development. Fluency development involves becoming fluent with what is already known, and there needs to be fluency development focuses in each of the four skills of listening, speaking, reading and writing. Although fluency development involves working with what is known and familiar, it can result in new learning, largely through the need to re-structure what is known so that it can be accessed and produced fluently. As a result of fluency development activities, we would expect frequent complex words to be stored as whole units rather than be reanalysed or recreated each time they are met or produced. We would also expect the application of rule-based morphological knowledge to be more fluently applied. A teacher needs to ensure that learners do easy extensive listening and reading for fluency development and do a speed reading course in a controlled vocabulary (see Sonia Millett's website: www.victoria.ac.nz/lals/about/staff/sonia-millett). They should also do speaking fluency activities like 4/3/2, where learners deliver the same talk three times to three different learners with decreasing time, and writing fluency activities like 10 minute writing (Nation 2013b), where learners write as much as they can in a set time.

The three strands of meaning-focused input, meaning-focused output and fluency development are all message-focused and involve incidental learning. They should make up about three-quarters of the course time. The teacher's main task with these three strands is to make sure that they truly exist in a course and that they exist in appropriate amounts. They do not require any special features that emphasize morphological knowledge. They simply provide substantial opportunities for learning through genuine language use. Because of this, the following part of this chapter, which focuses on deliberate teaching and learning, may give the impression that most of the opportunities for learning the morphological system will come through deliberate study. However, the pedagogical message behind the four strands is that learning can occur without teaching. The major reason for giving an equal amount of time to each strand is to ensure that teaching, which is a part of language-focused learning, does not take time away from learning through language use. When teaching takes more than its fair share of time, teaching is actually having a negative effect on learning.

Let us now look in detail at how the language-focused learning strand applies to word parts. *'Learning can occur without teaching'.*

1.6   How to Give Deliberate Attention to Word Parts

The language-focused learning strand of a language course typically has four kinds of learning opportunities.

1. *Teachers teach.* The teacher or the coursebook provides information about language features and provides exercises that practise those features. This can also include interactive intensive reading.
2. *Learners study.* The learners individually or in pairs or groups study, memorize and analyse language features.
3. *Learners get feedback.* The teacher or other learners provide feedback about learning and language use.
4. *Teachers train the learners.* The teacher trains the learners in strategies that assist learning and language use.

These four kinds of learning opportunities provide a wide variety of ways of giving deliberate attention to word parts, ranging from decontextualized analysis to contextualized activities to the development of meta-linguistic awareness-based strategies. Such attention greatly deepens the quality of processing of vocabulary and strengthens and enriches vocabulary knowledge. Let us see how each of these four kinds of opportunities applies to morphological knowledge.

1.6.1 Teaching about Word Parts

To make use of word parts in listening and reading, learners need to be able to recognize word parts in words, be able to assign a meaning or function to them, and be able to see how they contribute to the meaning of the whole word.

Breaking known words into parts: The teacher chooses some words that the learners already know, writes them on the board, and then cuts them into parts. So, words such as *happiness, teacher, unhappy, singing, worker, pleased* are written on the board, and the teacher draws vertical lines to separate the parts: *happi | ness, teach | er, un | happy*. After doing a few, the teacher then gets the learners to help with the cutting and eventually gives them a list of words to cut while working in pairs. The feedback on the activity can include discussion of the meaning or function of the affixes. When doing this the teacher can gradually build up a list of the most common affixes that the learners can refer to.

This simple but very useful activity should systematically draw on a list of the most useful affixes such as that in Table 1.1. By having a list as guidance, the teacher can make sure that the most useful affixes are well covered. This activity should be regularly used during intensive reading, guided listening and vocabulary development sessions. It is worth using such activities to develop the basis of a strategy for word part analysis. The first step in the strategy would be to look for known complete words within the word when making a cut and isolate them. These complete words within a word can also be cut, but may not need to be if the meaning becomes clear after the first cut. For example, when analysing *inconsiderate*, if the learner can recognize and understand the word *considerate*, then just making the cut after *in-* may be enough.

Memorizing word parts: Learners need to know the meanings and functions of at least the most useful affixes. For example, they need to know that a teacher is someone who teaches because the *-er* suffix turns a verb into a noun indicating a person or thing that does something. Directly teaching this kind of information is not likely to be an effective way of helping learners understand and retain this, especially if several affixes are covered at the same time. Teaching several together may encourage interference between the affixes, with learners mixing up the forms and meanings. An effective way of avoiding interference is to deal with the affixes in known words and to deal with them as they happen to come up in reading texts or other material. What may seem obvious to a teacher, for example that *mileage*, *endless* and *careful* are complex words with already known bases, may not be obvious to a learner.

There is a pair learning activity that can be used to help deliberate memorization. One learner in a pair is given the role of teacher and the other takes the role of learner. A sheet of affixes, meanings and examples like the one below is used by the learner taking the role of teacher. The examples in column three should be words the learners already know.

Affix	*Meaning/function*	*Examples*
-ness	makes a noun	happiness, slowness
un–	not	unhappy, uneven
-ly	makes an adverb	slowly, quietly
-er	a person or thing that does	teacher, roller
-less	without something	careless, hopeless
non–	not	nonsmoking, nonstop
-able	can be done	doable, drinkable
-ish	makes an adjective	selfish, childish
-y	makes an adjective	smoky, thirsty
-th	makes a number showing order	fifth, twentieth
-like	shows similarity	childlike, crablike
-ation	makes a noun	organization, purification

The learner in each pair has a folded sheet so that only the list of meanings is seen. The teacher's sheet is not folded and so the teacher in each pair can see all the information. The learner sees this:

↳Cutting + isolating word parts.

Meaning/function
makes a noun
not
makes an adverb
a person or thing that does something
without
not
can be done
makes an adjective
makes an adjective
makes a number showing order
shows similarity
makes a noun

The teacher chooses any affix on the sheet and says the affix and a word containing it from column three – '-*ly slowly*'. The learner looks down the list of meanings and tries to choose the correct meaning. If she does not choose the right meaning, the teacher says 'No, try again!' and repeats the affix and example word. If after three attempts the learner does not choose the right meaning, the teacher says '-ly makes an adverb' from column two, and then randomly chooses another affix to test, for example '*un- uneven*'. If the learner chooses the right meaning, the teacher says 'Good, well done!' and then revises the previous affix -ly by saying '-ly *slowly*'. In this way the teacher works through the items on the sheet in an unpredictable order, being careful to always revise all the previously tested items and giving praise when the answers are correct. This activity takes around 15 minutes and usually results in both the teachers and learners learning the items. About a week later, the learners should quickly do the same activity again to ensure that the learning is retained.

There is a very simple blank-filling activity which can be used to practise breaking words into parts and learning the meanings of the parts. Here is an example. The first example has been answered.

A worker is someone who <u>works</u>.
A teacher is someone who _____.
If you walk slowly, you walk in a _____ way.
When you do your work carefully, you do it in a _____ way.

This activity focuses on receptive knowledge of word parts in that the derived word is given and the learner needs to analyse to find the base. A follow-up version of this activity uses sentences like these to develop productive knowledge. The learner needs to recall a possible affix and make a derived word.

What would you call someone who teaches? <u>A teacher</u>
My friend eats a lot of pies. He's a very good pie _____.
He's very happy. What is the reason for his _____.

1.6.2   Studying Word Parts

If learners have a list of the most useful word parts, they can take responsibility for their own learning of them. Teachers should train learners in the use of the flash-card strategy (Nation 2013b: 99–102), making use of retrieval, spaced repetition and memory tricks. Learners can then use this strategy, putting an affix and example sentence on one side of a card and its meaning on the other to learn affixes. Flash-cards are a very effective way of deliberately learning vocabulary and it is a good idea to mix word learning and affix learning in the same pack of cards.

pre-   before

1.6.3   *Learning from Feedback*

Feedback is especially useful in learning inflectional suffixes. There is a remedial procedure that can be used to guide the conscious use of the plural suffix. It involves the following steps and should be applied initially as the result of feedback on written work.

If feedback indicates an error related to article usage or the noun group, ask yourself the following questions. In a feedback system for writing (see Nation 2013b: 112–14) such errors are indicated by a capital A in the margin with the relevant word in the same line underlined.

1. Is the noun countable or uncountable in this sentence? [If it is uncountable, it cannot take the plural form. If it is countable ask yourself the next question.]
2. Do I mean one or more than one? [If I mean one, make sure it does not have the plural form, and make sure it has *a*, *the* or a similar word in front of it. If I mean more than one, make sure the noun has the plural form.]

Being able to answer these questions requires practice and previous learning, including learning the countable/uncountable distinction, learning plural forms and learning which words like *a*, *the*, *one*, *each*, *every*, *this*, *that*, *my* and *John's* can come in front of singular countable nouns. Learning this procedure suits older learners, especially those who expect direct grammar instruction to be part of a language course.

There is a similar kind of self-checking procedure that can be used to check if a verb form is finite or non-finite. This is a first step to deciding whether the verb form needs to be marked for third person singular, or for past tense. The question to ask is, if I change the person or the time, does the verb need to change? If it does, then the decision needs to be made whether the time intended is present or past.

In a marking feedback system for written work, this kind of error can be indicated by a capital T (for tense) in the margin of the written work, and underlining in the text.

The goal of these self-checking procedures is to give the learner independence from the teacher in error correction and to try to bring about grammatical and morphological change through understanding. It is just one kind of approach to error correction.

1.6.4   *Strategy Training*

As soon as learners know some complex English words, within the first few months of learning English, there should be consciousness-raising directed at seeing the parts in words and at becoming aware of members of word families. The amount of attention given to this consciousness-raising will depend on the age of the learners and whether their first language also contains similar morphological processes. Consciousness-raising activities can include cutting familiar words into parts, and grouping members into word families (van Hees & Nation 2017).

Word parts, in particular derivational affixes, can be used to help newly met words stick in memory. The word part strategy involves using known parts to analyse new words to see how the meanings of the parts relate to the meaning of the word. The word part strategy is not a way of guessing the meaning of unfamiliar words. Using word parts to guess works only some of the time and needs to be used with caution. The word part strategy has the following steps.

1. Find the meaning of the new word by any available means such as looking it up in a dictionary.
2. Break the new word into parts, giving particular attention to prefixes.
3. Try to restate the meaning of the word using the meaning of the word parts.

For example, the word *prearranged* can be broken into the parts *pre-/arrange/-ed*. *Pre-* is a very useful prefix to know because it is usually easy to recognize, carries a clear meaning and occurs in a lot of words. The dictionary meaning of *prearranged* may be 'to arrange in advance'. If the prefix *pre-* has been learned as meaning 'before', then the meaning of *prearrange* can be simply restated as 'to arrange before'. This linking of the meaning of the word part to the meaning of the whole word makes it more memorable, most likely because of the increased number of associations with the word and its linking of new knowledge to existing knowledge.

The prerequisite knowledge for the word part strategy is (1) knowledge of the most useful prefixes (around twenty of these is a good starting point), (2) the well-practised skill of breaking words into parts, and (3) practice in restating the meanings of words to include the meanings of the prefixes. This strategy deserves regular practice in class time because it can be applied to large numbers of words.

This strategy can also make use of word bases. Wei and Nation (2013) provide lists of the most productive word bases, such as *spec* ('see'), *pos* ('put'), *vers* ('turn') and *ven* ('come'). There is the danger of over-analysis however. A cartridge has nothing to do with a cart, a category is not a bloody tomcat, and laterally has nothing to do with doing things later. The word part strategy involves checking the meaning of the word first to ensure there is a connection, and this checking can help avoid over-analysis.

When the first language of the learners is related to English, especially with Romance languages, there is the opportunity to use cognates as aids in word part analysis and synthesis. For example, Spanish speakers meeting words such as *beneficial* or *malicious* already have assistance from their first language in figuring out the English word. False friends, where there seems to be a helpful connection but there is not one, can be a problem, but they make up a small proportion of cross-language connections. Learners should be encouraged to use their first language knowledge of morphological principles and cognates to support their learning and use of English. If all the learners in a class share the same first language, there is value in spending a little time looking at morphology in that language and considering how this knowledge can support the learning of English.

Nw + Nation 2013

We have looked at a wide range of ways to give deliberate attention to word parts, to develop meta-linguistic awareness of morphology, and to encourage a strategic approach to dealing with complex words in use. However, teachers need to ensure that this deliberate attention fits within the one-quarter of the course time given to language-focused learning, and that three-quarters of the course time is given to language use.

1.7   Testing Knowledge of Morphology

As the vocabulary size of a learner of English as a foreign language increases, their knowledge of affixes also increases (Mochizuki & Aizawa 2000; Schmitt & Meara 1997), but their knowledge can be very patchy and does not follow the order of affixes in Bauer and Nation's (1993) levels.

Morphological knowledge can be tested for receptive use or productive use. Schmitt and Zimmermann (2002) examined productive knowledge using the following format.

Coherent

Noun: The judge was impressed by the _____ of the lawyer's argument.
Verb: The lawyer makes sure her points _____ with one another.
Adjective: The lawyer made _____ arguments.
Adverb: The lawyer argued _____.

The learners had to write in the appropriate derived form or put an X to indicate there was no appropriate form. This is a demanding test and learners averaged around 2 out of 4 correct. Schmitt and Meara's (1997) productive test was even more demanding in that a context was not provided and the learners had to decide which affixes each word could join with.

Mochizuki and Aizawa (2000) used a multiple-choice format. For prefixes, the prefix was attached to three nonsense bases and a choice of four prefix meanings was provided.

post-jax post-franulate poststrith   ↳ *refer to these*
(1) after (2) between (3) before (4) both   *studies in methods*

Suffixes were tested similarly with three example words and four part of speech choices. Nonsense bases were used so that learners could not use knowledge of whole words they had met previously but had to rely solely on affix knowledge.

Sasao and Webb (2017) developed the Word Part Levels Test to measure three kinds of word part knowledge – recognition of written affix forms, knowledge of affix meanings and knowledge of the syntactic properties of affixes. The test used the following three item types.

(1) sal- (2) cau- (3) lin- (4) dis- (The test-takers need to indicate which of the four forms is an affix. There is a set of similar items for suffixes.)

1. fore- (forewarn; foresee)
    (1) bad
    (2) in advance
    (3) person
    (4) many

2. -ment (development; management)
    (1) Noun
    (2) Verb
    (3) Adjective
    (4) Adverb

The test examines 118 different affixes and was trialled on over 1,700 different learners of English as a foreign language. As a result of the testing, the researchers were able to provide a list of the affixes ranked according to their likelihood of being known by EFL learners. The test and data are available from http://ysasaojp.info/testen.html.

McLean (2018) argues that the kind of knowledge measured by previous research using multiple-choice items and items asking students to identify the part of speech an affix creates does not truly represent the knowledge needed for reading comprehension. He argues that we need to focus on how learners cope with the derived forms they meet. McLean provided learners with sentences containing affixed words and then asked them to translate the underlined word into Japanese (see also Ward & Chuenjundaeng 2009).

The computer is now <u>usable</u> = _____

The bases were all high frequency words and the learners' knowledge of these bases was checked.

Tests of affix knowledge generally show that learners' knowledge of affixes is patchy and support the idea that some deliberate focus on morphology would be a useful addition to a language course. Although there is evidence that as vocabulary size increases, affix knowledge increases, the returns for some deliberate well-targeted work on morphology are likely to be high and could speed up the learning of this pervasive aspect of language knowledge.

1.8 Applying the Knowledge Found in this Book

In the following chapters of this book, detailed practical information is given about particular affixes. This information is given to help teachers and learners make sensible decisions about where to focus deliberate attention, what to be careful about and what not to be concerned about.

This information needs to be considered against the background of the four strands, and frequency information. Learning can occur without deliberate teaching or learning, and a lot of the low frequency affixes and uses of affixes can be learned through meeting them in normal language use. Some items and rules however are very frequent and may also be readily learned through giving them deliberate attention (this is particularly true of the inflectional suffixes). Such items and rules are clearly signalled in this book.

Teachers and very advanced learners with an interest in the morphology of English will find value in reading systematically through the book. It will also be a particularly useful resource for teachers and learners who want to know the most important rules and items to give their attention to, and for teachers and learners who are puzzled by certain uses and exceptions. To help those interested in particular items, the book has a substantial index, and throughout the book there are clear signals marking important features and items. The book should also be of value to those involved in the production of teaching materials and in language curriculum design.

References

Anglin, J. M. 1993. Vocabulary development: a morphological analysis. *Monographs of the Society for Research in Child Development* 58 (10 Serial No. 238), 1–165.

Bauer, L. & I. S. P. Nation. 1993. Word families. *International Journal of Lexicography* 6(4), 253–279.

Hees, J. van & I. S. P. Nation. 2017. *What every primary school teacher should know about vocabulary*. Wellington: NZCER Press.

McLean, S. 2018. Evidence for the adoption of the flemma as an appropriate word counting unit. *Applied Linguistics* 39(6), 823–845.

Mochizuki, M. & K. Aizawa. 2000. An affix acquisition order for EFL learners: an exploratory study. *System* 28, 291–304.

Nagy, W. E. & R. C. Anderson. 1984. How many words are there in printed school English? *Reading Research Quarterly* 19(3), 304–330.

Nation, I. S. P. 2007. The four strands. *Innovation in Language Learning and Teaching* 1(1), 1–12.

Nation, I. S. P. 2013a. *Learning vocabulary in another language*. 2nd edn. Cambridge. Cambridge University Press.

Nation, I. S. P. 2013b. *What should every EFL teacher know?* Seoul: Compass Publishing.

Nation, I. S. P. 2016. *Making and using word lists for language learning and testing*. Amsterdam: John Benjamins.

Sasao, Y. & S. Webb. 2017. The word part levels test. *Language Teaching Research* 21(1), 12–30.

Schmitt, N. & C. Zimmerman. 2002. Derivative word forms: what do learners know? *TESOL Quarterly* 36(2), 145–171.

Schmitt, N. & P. Meara. 1997. Researching vocabulary through a word knowledge framework: word associations and verbal suffixes. *Studies in Second Language Acquisition* 19, 17–36.

Ward, J. & J. Chuenjundaeng. 2009. Suffix knowledge: acquisition and applications. *System* 37, 461–469.

Webb, S. & P. Nation. 2017. *How vocabulary is learned*. Oxford: Oxford University Press.

Wei, Z. 2015. Does teaching mnemonics for vocabulary learning make a difference? Putting the keyword method and the word part technique to the test. *Language Teaching Research* 19(1), 43–69.

Wei, Z. & P. Nation. 2013. The word part technique: a very useful vocabulary teaching technique. *Modern English Teacher* 22(1), 12–16.

2
ASSUMPTIONS

This book deals with the morphology of English from the point of view of the non-native learner of English, and those involved in teaching that learner and developing materials for that learner. That is, it deals with the form of words, but it does not deal with the ways in which the forms are used. For example, it will talk about the ways to form the plural of nouns in English, but will not tell you that after the phrase *More than one* you will need a singular form rather than a plural form. We say *More than one man has been seen in the vicinity* rather than ★*More than one men have been seen in the vicinity*.

Even in this first paragraph, we have started to use some notational conventions to allow us to be more concise and more precise in what we say. The asterisk used just above is a way of indicating that what follows is not a good piece of English. Italics, such as were used to mark the two sentences in the last sentence of the previous paragraph, will be used to show words or other pieces of language that we are citing as examples. This means that

> *Spaghetti* is red

is true if and only if the word *spaghetti* is set in red type, while

> Spaghetti is red

is true if and only if there is some pasta which is coloured red. Other notational devices will be introduced as we go along, and they are summarized in a table at the front of the book. Some of the notational devices are our own, but many of them are standard usage in linguistic study.

We have tried to make the presentation as straightforward as possible, but there is a certain amount of linguistic knowledge that we have presupposed on the part of the reader.

First, we have assumed that readers can distinguish the various word-classes or parts of speech. In particular, we use *adjective, adverb, noun, preposition* and *verb* freely, and assume that these will be understood.

Secondly, we assume that readers are familiar with terms for morphological categories such as *third person singular, tense, plural, past participle* and so on. Where derivational morphology is concerned, we are rather more explicit about what we understand by our terms. We tend to avoid the terms *inflection* and *derivation*, but the book is organized according to these categories, and we assume they are also understood at a superficial level.

Although we present a transcription system in Chapter 3, and introduce a number of phonological terms in that chapter, we assume that readers can read a transcription and are familiar with phonological categories such as plosive, syllable and stress.

Most importantly, we assume that readers know about *affixes* (*prefixes* and *suffixes*), and we term what these affixes can be attached to *bases*.

An assumption that is not specifically about morphological structure is about the uniformity of the English language. In general terms we assume that the English language is uniform wherever it is spoken. This is often not true. Sometimes it is so untrue that we are forced to comment on it. However, we cannot comment in detail about every single case of potential variation, not only because in some cases the information is simply not available, but also because in other instances it would take too much space for very little reward. Nevertheless, where we believe that a major correlation of the variation is that one form is found more generally in the United States and another is found more generally in Britain, we say so. We are often following standard commentaries when we say this, occasionally we are following our own experience. Such generalizations, though, are just that – they are generalizations. Some forms marked as American will be found in Britain, some forms marked as British will be found in the United States, and forms marked as either may be found in Canada. Such areal marking, therefore, should always be taken as indicative rather than as definitive. It always means 'we believe that this form is preferred on one side of the Atlantic or the other' and never 'this form is found on one side of the Atlantic to the total exclusion of the other'. American forms are often increasing in usage in Britain (and so heard more frequently from younger speakers), and can be found in countries such as Australia, which otherwise might be expected to prefer a British alternative. Similarly, pronunciations other than the ones we give may be heard from native speakers of English. We do not give unjustified pronunciations, but neither can we give every possible pronunciation of everything: providing twenty or more pronunciations of some words would not help our readers.

3

SOUND AND SPELLING

3.1 Introduction

In English it is frequently the case that the spelling of a word does not directly reflect its pronunciation. A standard example would be that *night* and *knight* sound exactly the same, and that *through* and *blue* rhyme. At the same time *through* and *rough* do not rhyme. The result is that we need to be very clear about when we are dealing with the spelling system and when we are dealing with the sound system. An English word can start *kn-* if we are talking about the spelling system, but not if we are talking about the sound system. We will use two mechanisms to keep them apart. The first is that we will enclose sounds in square brackets: *knight* starts with [n]. In contrast we will enclose letters in angle brackets: *knight* starts with <kn>. The second is that we will draw a distinction between consonant sounds and consonant letters, and equally between vowel sounds and vowel letters. We will not talk about 'consonants' and 'vowels' in isolation. Sometimes we will abbreviate consonant sound to Cs and consonant letter to CL, and similarly vowel sound will be abbreviated to Vs and vowel letter to VL.

3.2 Sounds

The sounds of every dialect of English are different, sometimes just a little bit different, sometimes very different. When we mark pronunciations in this book, we use a notation for the pronunciation of the standard English used in southern England, sometimes called 'RP' (short for 'received pronunciation') and sometimes called 'Oxford English'. This system should be perfectly interpretable for learners of Australian or New Zealand English or South African English, but not for learners of North American dialects of English, or Scottish and Irish dialects of English, who will need to make some adjustments.

3.2.1 Consonant Sounds

The consonant sounds of English are laid out in Table 3.1, along with a classification of those sounds and some examples of each in word-initial and word-final position (where they occur in these positions).

The sounds that are <u>underlined</u> are plosives; the sounds marked in (circles) are fricatives; the sounds marked in **bold** are nasals. The plosives, fricatives and [ʧ] and [ʤ] as a class are called obstruents. The sounds [s, z, ʃ, ʒ, ʧ, ʤ] are classed as sibilants, and are important for the occurrence of certain affixes. The sound [r] is shown not to occur word-finally. There are many dialects of English, both inside the United Kingdom and beyond it, where there is a final [r] in a word like *far*. But that is not the case in standard southern English, where *far* and *shah* rhyme. The sound [ʒ] occurs initially only in a few foreign words like *gendarme*.

3.2.2 Vowel Sounds

The vowel sounds of English are laid out in Table 3.2, along with a partial classification and an example of a word containing each sound. All the vowels are illustrated in a stressed syllable except for [i] and [ə], which occur only in unstressed positions.

TABLE 3.1 English consonant sounds

	Voiceless sounds			Voiced sounds		
	Sound	Initial example	Final example	Sound	Initial example	Final example
Bilabial	p̲	pie	cap	b̲	buy	cab
				m	my	ram
Labio-dental	(f)	fie	fife	(v)	vie	five
Dental	(θ)	thigh	sheath	(ð)	thy	sheathe
Alveolar	t̲	tie	bat	d̲	die	bad
	(s)	suc	bus	(z)	zoo	buzz
				n	nigh	ran
				l	lie	file
				r̲	rye	–
Post-alveolar	ʧ	cheap	batch	ʤ	Jeep	badge
	(ʃ)	shy	rash	(ʒ)	–	beige
Palatal				j	you	–
Velar	k̲	coal	rack	g̲	goal	rag
				ŋ	–	rang
Glottal	(h)	high	–			
Labial-velar				w	why	–

TABLE 3.2 English vowel sounds

	Front	Example	Central	Example	Back	Example
Short						
	ɪ	pit			ʊ	put
	e	pet				
	æ	pat			ɒ	pot
			ʌ	putt		
			ə	putter		
	i	putty				
Long						
	iː	bead			uː	booed
			ɜː	bird	ɔː	board
					ɑː	bard
Diphthongs						
	eɪ	bay				
	aɪ	buy			ɔɪ	boy
	ɪə	beer			ʊə	boor
	eə	bear				
			əʊ	beau		
			aʊ	bough		

The long and short vowels that are not diphthongs are monophthongs. The monophthongs underlined are rounded; rounding only applies to elements of diphthongs. Diphthongs are long vowels.

3.2.3 Stress

In any English word which contains more than one syllable, one of the syllables is stronger, more prominent, than the others when the word is spoken in isolation. The terminology surrounding this is very variable, but here we will say that the syllable is stressed. In words of one syllable spoken in isolation, the sole syllable is stressed. The stressed syllable in polysyllabic words is marked here with a preceding stress mark, so that *billow* is transcribed ['bɪləʊ] and *below* is transcribed [bɪ'ləʊ]. Stress is marked in transcriptions where it is relevant.

The system of stress in English is extremely complex, and there are several distinct views on how many different levels of stress are needed for a good description. Since we are dealing with morphology rather than with phonology here, we will deal with just three levels: stress (which we can call primary stress, to distinguish it from), secondary stress and lack of stress (that is in unstressed syllables). Secondary stressed syllables have full vowel quality: they contain one of the vowels from Table 3.2 that is not [ə] or [i]. Unstressed syllables contain one of the vowels [ə] or [i], or sometimes no vowel at all, in words like *button* and *bottle*, which may be ['bʌtn] and ['bɒtl], each two syllables with only a consonant in the second syllable. For some speakers, the vowels [ɪ] and [ʊ] may be unstressed sometimes, as in *prefer* [prɪˈfɜː] and *thank you* [ˈθæŋk jʊ]. In the word *condescend* [kɒndɪˈsend], the last syllable is stressed (or carries primary stress), the first syllable has secondary stress and the second syllable is unstressed (and for some speakers contains the vowel [ə]).

3.3   Spelling Rules

S1   <y> becomes <ie> before a suffix beginning with a Cʟ, unless Vʟ + <y> spell the vowel sound.

Examples:
rely + s > relies
jelly + s > jellies
boy + s > boys
buoy + s > buoys

S2   <y> becomes <i> before a suffix, unless Vʟ + <y> spell a vowel sound.

Examples:
deny + -ed > denied
deny + -al > denial
happy + -ness > happiness
boy + -hood > boyhood
easy + -ly > easily

Exception: busy + -ness > busyness (because *business* is now a separate word)
    Where this would result in a sequence of <ii>, one of the <i>s is deleted.

Examples:
anthology + ize > anthologize
neology + ism > neologism

S3   If a word ends with a stressed syllable and that syllable contains a short vowel sound and a final consonant sound written as a single consonant letter, that consonant letter is doubled before a suffix beginning with a vowel letter.

Examples:
sin + -ing > sinning
red + -en > redden
pat + -ed > patted
repel + -ing > repelling
Exception:
bus + -es > buses

EXPLANATORY NOTE

This is the version of the rule for writing American English, since this version is more regular than the British version. The British version is inconsistent as to whether the final syllable of the word must be stressed or not. So in the traditional British spelling (now less commonly used) *focus* + *-ing* > *focussing* (despite the fact that the final syllable of *focus* is unstressed, but the doubling still occurs because the last vowel sound in the word is not [ə]), but *fathom* + *-ed* > *fathomed* with no doubling (*fathom* is stressed on the first syllable and has [ə] as its last vowel).

S4 A final silent <e> is deleted before a suffix beginning with a vowel letter or a <y> pronounced as a vowel sound.

Examples:
come + –ing > coming
dine + –ing > dining
live + –ing > living
stone + –y > stony
state + –ed > stated
divine + –ity > divinity (note the vowel change in the pronunciation here)
wide + –en > widen
Exceptions:
acre + –age > acreage
game + –y > gamey

S5 If a word ends in the letter <a> and a suffix begins with the letter <a>, one of the <a>s is deleted.

Examples:
Africa + –an > African
medulla + –ary > medullary
pleura + –al > pleural
trivia + –al > trivial

S6 If a word ends in <er >, delete the <e> before a suffix beginning with a <y> pronounced as a vowel.

Examples:
anger + –y > angry
hunger + y > hungry

3.4   Sound Rules

P1   The letter <c> when it is final in a base, and especially when it is part of the suffix -ic, is pronounced [s] before the suffixes -ic/-ical, -ify, -ize, -ism, -ist, -ity.

Examples:
electric + -ity > electri[s]ity
historic + -ism > histori[s]ism
lyric + -ist > lyri[s]ist
Exceptions:
zinc + -ic > zin[k]ic

P2   When a word containing a suffix which starts with a vowel sound has an [r] immediately before that vowel sound, that [r] is silent when the base is said in isolation.

Examples:
covering [ˈkʌvərɪŋ] is related to [ˈkʌvə]
burglary [ˈbɜːgləri] is related to [ˈbɜːglə]
lustrous [ˈlʌstrəs] is related to [ˈlʌstə]
bearer [ˈbeərə] is related to [beə]
choleric [kɒˈlerɪk] is related to [ˈkɒlə]

Comment: This is not true in standard North American forms of English, nor in Scottish or Irish English, where the final [r] is maintained.

P3   When a [ə] appears before [r] or [l] with the consonant followed by an affix that begins with a Vs, the [ə] is often deleted, and sometimes obligatorily deleted. Where both pronunciations are found, the one without the [ə] is informal or colloquial.

Examples:
clever + -er > cleverer [ˈklevərə] or [ˈklevrə]
anger + -y > angry [ˈæŋgri]
radical + -ly > radically [ˈrædɪkəli] or [ˈrædɪkli]
nature + -al > natural [ˈnætʃərəl] or [ˈnætʃrəl] (note the vowel shortening)
slender + -er > slenderer [ˈslendərə] or [ˈslendrə]
Exceptions:
terror + ist > terrorist [ˈterərɪst]

Helps with tutorial rationale even though spelling wasn't explicitly covered

4

PLURALS OF NOUNS

4.1 The Regular Case

Rule – spelling:
Add <es> after <s, z, sh, ch, x> and sometimes after final <o>.
Otherwise add <s>.

Rule – sound:
After a sibilant consonant sound, add [ɪz].
After any other voiceless consonant sound, add [s].
Everywhere else, add [z].

Examples – spelling:
princess > princesses, waltz > waltzes, marsh > marshes, match > matches, box > boxes, tomato > tomatoes

Examples – sound:
gas [gæs] > [gæsɪz], rose [rəʊz] > [rəʊzɪz], rush [rʌʃ] > [rʌʃɪz], match [mætʃ] > [mætʃɪz], judge [dʒʌdʒ] > [dʒʌdʒɪz], faith [feɪθ] > [feɪθs], cap [kæp] > [kæps], cat [kæt] > [kæts], cake [keɪk] > [keɪks], cuff [kʌf] > [kʌfs], dog [dɒg] > [dɒgz], son [sʌn] > [sʌnz], hotel [həʊˈtel] > [həʊˈtelz], cow [kaʊ] > [kaʊz]

LEVEL
This rule is required at the earliest stages of learning English.
    S3 on consonant letter doubling applies but not very helpfully.

Since <sh> can never double, consonant letter doubling applies only to word-final <s> and <z>, since these are the only cases where a vowel letter is added after the base.

Words with final <s>. The rule fails to apply in most of these cases, but only *bus* and *gas* are frequent enough to be worth consideration.

as	asses ('Roman weight'), aesir ('Norse god')
bus	buses
cos	? no plural: use *cos lettuces* or *cosines*, as relevant
crus	crura
gas	gases *or* gasses
jus	jus
nis	nisses
pus	no plural
sis	no plural
vas	rarely plural, but has an irregular plural *vasa*

Words with final <z>. There are very few nouns that end in a stressed syllable with a final single <z>, and of those the only common one is *quiz*, which obeys the rule. The plural of *fez* can be written with one or two <z>s. *Swiz* is often written with <zz> in the singular, and so <zz> is expected.

S1 on replacing <y> with <ie> applies.

Examples:

assembly	assemblies
city	cities
country	countries
delivery	deliveries
enquiry	enquiries
lily	lilies
monopoly	monopolies
orderly	orderlies
philosophy	philosophies
sky	skies
EXCEPTION	
poly (= polytechnic)	polys

POTENTIAL DIFFICULTIES

For speakers of languages that allow no (or only limited) word-final consonant sounds (languages such as Chinese, Italian, Japanese, Vietnamese), adding a final consonant sound may be difficult in speech.

Where a final [s] or [z] makes a final cluster of consonant sounds, these may be particularly difficult to pronounce. Examples: *ends, facts, lamps, roasts, texts.*

For speakers of some languages where plurality is not overtly marked on nouns, remembering to use the plural form, especially when it is redundant, as in *three pencils*, may be difficult.

4.2   Umlaut Plurals

Umlaut is a change in vowel due to a historical process which can no longer be seen. The following plural forms with the relevant vowel change simply have to be learnt.

Singular		*Plural*	
foot	/fʊt/	feet	/fiːt/
goose	/guːs/	geese	/giːs/
louse	/laʊs/	lice	/laɪs/
man	/mæn/	men	/men/
mouse	/maʊs/	mice	/maɪs/
tooth	/tuːθ/	teeth	/tiːθ/
woman	/wʊmən/	women	/wɪmɪn/

There are regularities here in terms of spelling (fewer with reference to the pronunciation), but the generalizations do not cover enough forms to make it worthwhile learning them.

LEVEL
These plurals have to be recognized and used from the earliest stages of English language learning.

> ADVICE: Regular plurals for some of these words may be heard occasionally, but except in a very few cases will sound childish. Even advanced learners can always use the umlaut plural forms. The use of umlaut plurals with other nouns (with the possible exception of *mongoose*) is always jocular (e.g. *spice* as the plural of *spouse*).

4.3   Plurals with Voicing of the Last Base Consonant Sound

A small number of nouns which end with a voiceless fricative sound, voice that fricative before adding the relevant regular plural marker.

The only noun ending in [s] to do this regularly is *house*, with the plural form [haʊzɪz]. Even this noun is not always irregular: in Scottish and some varieties of North American English a regular form with [s] is heard.

Most nouns ending in [f] keep the [f] in the plural. Some, however, voice it to [v]. This is indicated in the spelling.

These words always change [f] to [v] (and <f(e)> to <ve>) in the plural: *calf, elf, knife, life, loaf, sheaf, shelf, thief, wife, wolf.*

These words vary as to whether they have a regularly formed plural with an [f] or a plural with a [v]; spellings with <f> or with <v> are found: *behalf, dwarf, half, hoof, roof, scarf, wharf.*

All other words in [f], whether that is spelt <f>, <ff> or <ph>, have regular plurals.

Most nouns ending in [θ] have regular plurals. Because there is often no distinction in spelling between [θ] and [ð] in plurals, speakers vary a lot in which words they include in the class.

These words always have a plural with [ð]: *booth* (which is relevant only for those who pronounce it [buːθ] – some pronounce it [buːð]), *mouth, youth* ('young man').

These words sometimes have a plural with [ð]: *lath, oath, path, sheath, truth, wreath.*

ADVICE: Learn the words which must take a [v] plural, and the word *mouth.*

At advanced levels, note that some of the variable plurals carry social value: *roofs* is prescribed, even though most speakers seem to prefer *rooves.*

Of the variable [θ] words, *path* is the one that you are most likely to hear with [ð].

4.4   N-plurals

Three words have a plural form ending in <n>. They are listed below.

brother (in the religious sense)	brethren or brothers
child	children
ox	oxen

At advanced levels you may hear a few other words with an <n> plural, but they are always jocular or otherwise stylistically marked.

LEVEL
Children has to be used from the earliest stage in learning English. There is no alternative to *oxen*, but it is rare these days in urban societies.

4.5   Regular Plurals of Nouns Ending in <o>

Some nouns ending in <o> have a plural form with <es>, others have a plural form with <s>. Many words allow both forms.

Words which must have an <es> plural are: *bubo, domino* (the game), *echo, go, hero, negro* (which is a taboo word, these days), *potato, tomato, torpedo, veto.*

Words which may have an <es> plural are: *archipelago, banjo, buffalo, cargo, desperado, domino* (the mask), *flamingo, fresco, grotto, halo, hobo, innuendo, mango, motto, no, peccadillo, salvo, volcano, zero.*

All other words ending in <o>, which includes all words ending in <oo>, take a regular <s> plural.

> ADVICE: Learn the words that must take <es>, and add <s> to all the others. Many of the words that must take <es> are relatively rare, and will not be needed at elementary levels.

4.6 Unmarked Plurals

Some plural nouns have no markers of the plural at all. There are various different types here, and there is a lot of variation as to whether regular plurals co-exist with the unmarked plural.

4.6.1 Words Which Refer to a Collective

Words which refer to sets of individuals may not take a plural marker but take plural concord. These include *cattle, offspring, police, swine*; the descriptions of people of certain nationalities, including many with the suffix *-ese* including *Chinese, Japanese, Maltese, Portuguese, Swiss, Vietnamese*; the names of various native peoples (these nearly always have the possibility of regular forms as well), such as *Apache, Bantu, Inuit, Maori, Navajo.*

4.6.2 Words Referring to Animals

The most common types here are *deer* and *sheep*, though regular plurals may sometimes be heard with *deer*.

Animals which are hunted for commercial exploitation often have unmarked plurals, especially words like *antelope, bison, mink, moose*. Regular plurals are used when the meaning 'types of ~' is intended.

4.6.3 Words Referring to Birds

Birds that are hunted as game are particularly prone to having unmarked plurals. This includes words such as *duck, grouse, pheasant, pigeon, quail*. Ducks in a pond or the farmyard are likely to get the regular plural, as are pigeons in the street or in a coop. When the plural means 'types of ~', the regular plural is used.

4.6.4   Words Referring to Fish

The word *fish* itself is usually found with an unmarked plural, but can have a regular plural in circumstances which are not clear. When *fish* is the second element in a compound (*crayfish*, *dogfish*, etc.) the unmarked plural is particularly likely, especially if these species are regarded as commercial catch. Other kinds of fish vary considerably, but *cod, plaice, salmon, snapper, trout* are regularly found with an unmarked plural, while *anchovy, eel, herring, mackerel, sardine* usually have a regular plural. Other kinds of sea-food usually take regular plurals: *clams, lobsters, oysters, scallops. Shrimp* may be treated as uncountable, but may also have a regular or an unmarked plural.

4.6.5   Other Words

The word *craft* and its compounds (*aircraft, water craft*) usually have an unmarked plural.

The word *dice* is usually treated as either singular or plural, but there is an old-fashioned usage whereby the singular is *die*.

Some old-fashioned slang words for British money like *bob, quid* usually had an unmarked plural. This may be because they are usually preceded by numbers. Expressions like *six foot two* (six foot, two inches (tall)) may also show a singular form despite the clearly plural meaning. There is widespread but sporadic use of singular forms of other measures after numbers (*five mile, fifteen pound*), but these are not standard.

> ADVICE: Use regular plurals for all these words except *sheep* and *fish* until you have heard them used with unmarked plurals in context.

4.7   Foreign Plurals

English has borrowed a series of plural markers from other languages. They tend to be rare words which are used in formal registers, but a few of them are completely general. They are dealt with below according to the language from which the plural marker comes.

LEVEL
Because of the rarity of the words involved, these words are not needed at elementary levels, and very few of them are needed at intermediate level.

> ADVICE: With all these words use regular plurals unless you have heard them used with the foreign plural in your area of specialization.

4.7.1 Latin

There are four major patterns of plural marking from Latin, and then a number of marginal patterns. Of these four patterns, only the first has any vitality in English, and even that is limited.

Rule:

> **Change a final <us> in the singular to <i>.**
> **The pronunciation of the <i> varies between [iː] and [aɪ] in unpredictable ways.**

Examples:

alumnus	alumni	[əˈlʌmnaɪ]
hippopotamus	hippopotami	[hɪpəˈpɒtəmaɪ]
locus	loci	[ˈləʊkiː] ~ [ˈləʊsaɪ]
nucleus	nuclei	[ˈnjuːkliaɪ]
stimulus	stimuli	[ˈstimjʊliː]

Rule:

> **Change a final <a> in the singular to <ae>.**
> **The pronunciation of the <ae> varies between [iː] and [aɪ] in unpredictable ways.**

Examples:

amoeba	amoebae	[əˈmiːbiː]
antenna	antennae	[ænˈtenaɪ]
formula	formulae	[ˈfɔːmjʊliː]
vertebra	vertebrae	[ˈvɜtɪbriː], [vɜːtɪbreɪ]

Rule:

> **Change a final <um> in the singular to <a>, pronounced [ə].**

Examples:

bacterium	bacteria
datum	data
erratum	errata
forum	fora
millennium	millennia
stratum	strata

Rule:
Change a final <x> in the singular into <ces>.
The <ces> is pronounced [siːz].

Examples:
appendix	appendices
aviatrix	aviatrices
codex	codices
index	indices
matrix	matrices

There are also a number of Latin plurals which, as far as English is concerned, are simply irregular. These include the following:

corpus	corpora
genus	genera
larynx	larynges
opus	opera
species	species

4.7.2   Greek

There are two major patterns that come from Greek, and some very rare forms that are irregular.

Rule:
Change a final <on> in the singular to <a>, pronounced [ə].

Examples:
automaton	automata
criterion	criteria
phenomenon	phenomena

POTENTIAL PROBLEM: native speakers of English are very insecure about these nouns, and learners may hear plural forms used as singular forms, regular plurals or sheer inconsistency.

Rule:
Change a final <is> in the singular to <es>.
In pronunciation, replace [ɪs] with [iːz].

Examples:

basis	bases
crisis	crises
emphasis	emphases
hypothesis	hypotheses
parenthesis	parentheses
testis	testes
thesis	theses

As far as English is concerned, the following are simply irregular:

iris (in the eye)	irides *or* irises
stigma (in Christian theology)	stigmata

4.7.3 French

Most French plurals are marked with a final <s>, and these are just treated as though they are English. Two other patterns are transferred to English.

Words ending in <u> have an <x> added in the plural. The <x> is usually pronounced as [z].

Examples:

chateau	chateaux
milieu	milieux
plateau	plateaux
trousseau	trousseaux

Another set of French words shows no change in the spelling, but may show regular English plural pronunciation.

Examples:

chamois (window-cleaning cloth)	[ʃæmi]	chamois	[ʃæmiz]
chassis	[ʃæsi]	chassis	[ʃasiz]
corps	[kɔː]	corps	[kɔːz]
patois	[ˈpætwɑː]	patois	[ˈpætwɑːz]
rendez-vous	[ˈrɒndeɪvuː]	rendez-vous	[ˈrɒndeɪvuːz]

4.7.4 Hebrew

A very few nouns of Hebrew origin add the suffix -*im* in the plural.

Examples:

cherub	cherubim
goy	goyim

kibbutz	kibbutzim
seraph	seraphim

4.7.5 Italian

A number of Italian words in the fields of music, food and art history, which end in <o>, have a possible plural form in <i> in technical usage. This <i> is pronounced [iː].

Examples:

castrato	castrati
maestro	maestri
soprano	soprani
tempo	tempi

> POTENTIAL PROBLEM: Anyone who knows any Italian may have problems with Italian plurals in English, since many of them do not work in English as they do in Italian. *Spaghetti* and *tagliatelli*, for instance, plural nouns in Italian, are uncountable singular nouns in English; *panini* and *zucchini* are also singular in English. Italian feminine plurals in <e> do not appear to be regularly used in English. The plural of *pizza* is *pizzas*, not **pizze*, but the plural of *lira* (the former currency of Italy) was *lire* [liːrə] or [liːreɪ].

4.8 Plurals with an Apostrophe

In a few cases where the base the plural is added to is not considered to be a real noun, an apostrophe is added before the plural marker in writing, although there is nothing in the pronunciation to show this. Such uses of the apostrophe are increasingly old-fashioned, but may be found in texts.

Examples:
&'s
B+'s
if's and and's
mind your p's and q's
the 1970's

Another old-fashioned use is for an apostrophe to be used before the plural marker when the noun ends in a vowel letter other than <e>.

Examples:
guru's
piano's
toga's
wadi's

ADVICE: This usage should be avoided in current English.

4.9   Problems with Plurals

LEVEL
The material in this section is only needed at advanced levels.

There are a few places where different plural markers are used for different meanings of the noun. Speakers do not always agree about these, which may give rise to variation. Some examples are given below.

appendixes	'sections in a book'	appendices	'parts of the intestine'
cherubs	'small children'	cherubim	'angelic beings'
indexes	'sections in books', 'fingers'	indices	'mathematical ratios'
irises	'flowers' or 'parts of the eye'	irides	'parts of the eye'
stigmas	'disgraces'	stigmata	'marks on the body of Christ'
youths (/θs/)	'young ages'	youths (/ðz/)	'young men'

Some expressions borrowed from French are prescriptively expected to mark the plural on the first element, though in practice the whole construction may have the plural at its end.

Prescribed form	*Form also found*
courts martial	court martials
governors general	governor generals
heirs apparent	heir apparents (rare)
letters patent	

The same thing happens with some vocabulary items of the form N+P+N.

Prescribed form	*Form also found (especially in spoken language)*
maids-of-honour	
mothers-in-law	mother-in-laws
powers-of-attorney	power-of-attorneys (rare)

Some compounds which have *man* or *woman* in the first element showing gender show plural marking on both elements.

Examples:
gentlemen farmers
menservants
women doctors
women drivers

The usual case is for a complex noun to take the same plural marker as the form on the righthand edge of the word would normally take (or, if it is an element which would not normally have a plural form, the regular plural).

Examples:
Canada geese
cover-ups
forget-me-nots
harvest-mice
timber wolves

There are a number of nouns where the plural form is not settled in English. These are mainly nouns which may take either foreign or regular plural marking, such as *octopus* (where plurals *octopuses, octopi* and *octopodes* are found – and the first is recommended for foreign learners) or *court-martial* (already mentioned above). But as well as forms like *mother-in-law*, there are other points of dispute, often where the noun is interpreted figuratively or as a part of a name. Thus the plural of a *computer mouse* will probably be *computer mice*, but *computer mouses* is sometimes found; the plural of the Disney character *Mickey Mouse* is likely to be *Mickey Mouses*. The plural of *mongoose* is sometimes *mongeese* (by false analogy with *goose*, even though a *mongoose* is not a *goose*).

In unedited written English, the apostrophe is frequently used more often in the plural than is normatively accepted, and notices in shop windows such as *leg's of lamb* or *apple's* can be found, although learners should not emulate such usages.

4.10   Words with only Plural Form

Some nouns only have a plural form; most of these behave as ordinary plural nouns, in that they show plural agreement and cannot take the indefinite article *a/ an*. A few can take singular agreement, and a very few can take the indefinite article. There is some variation among speakers on which words fit into this category.

The first set of words to be considered is actually irrelevant, but looks relevant. It is made up of words ending in -*ics*. These look like plurals (and are historically plurals, based on Greek and Latin models), but in most cases are best treated as singular nouns formed from an adjective by an -*s* suffix. Thus terms like *econometrics, linguistics, mathematics, obstetrics, phonetics, physics, semantics*, which denote areas of study, take singular agreement: *Mathematics is at the core of all the sciences,* ★*Mathematics are at the core of all the sciences.* In some instances where the meaning is not an area of study, plural agreement may be found: *Politics have dominated the arguments, not logic; His ethics leave much to be desired.*

The most general rule is that nouns that look like plurals behave like plurals, whether there is a corresponding singular form or not. The following nouns with plural forms typically behave as plurals.

Examples:
(head)quarters
antipodes
arms
auspices
banns
binoculars
clothes
customs
dregs
genitals
goggles
guts
heads / tails
jeans
manners
outskirts
pliers
pyjamas (US: pajamas)
refreshments (the singular form is usually uncountable)
remains
scissors
suds

thanks
troops
tropics
trousers
tweezers

Some words have, in effect, two homophonous plurals, one which shows a regular plural meaning applied to a singular base, and another where the plural noun has a distinct meaning.

Examples of words with plural forms for certain meanings:

Noun	Regular meaning	Meaning when used only in the plural
bellow	'loud shout'	'mechanism for blowing air'
brief	'set of instructions'	'underpants'
compass	'device for indicating the north'	'device for drawing circles'
drawer	'one of a set of lidless boxes'	'underwear'
glass	'drinking vessel'	'spectacles'
look	'a glance'	'appearance'
scales	'parts of the skin of fish or reptiles'	'a balance'
spectacle	'grand sight'	'eye-wear'
trunk	'large piece of luggage'	'swimwear'
wit	'funny person'	'mental abilities'

The names for some diseases have an apparently plural form, but are often used with singular concord. How much they are used as singulars depends on the individual word and the variety of English concerned, but where there is prescription it is for singular concord.

Examples of words for diseases with plural form but potential singular concord:
hiccups
hives
measles
mumps
rickets
shingles

The same phenomenon can be found with names for some games, where singular concord is used for the game itself rather for the items used in the game.

Examples of words for games with plural form but singular concord:
cards
checkers (US)
darts
dominoes
draughts (Br)
ninepins
skittles

In some instances, the base of a noun with an -s looks like an adjective, and the
-s may be a derivational affix rather than a plural marker (as in the instances like
mathematics dealt with above).

Examples of adjective-based formations:

blues	'musical style'
commons	'ordinary people; food (now old-fashioned)'
goods	'freight'
greens	'vegetables'
news	'information on current events' Takes singular concord
odds	'chances'
riches	'wealth'
valuables	'valuable things'

In a very few cases, a noun that looks as though it might be plural can also
take the indefinite article *a/an*. The only cases where this is normal may be the
following:

innings (in cricket, and in figures of speech based on cricket)
scissors (a manoeuvre in rugby)

When these nouns with no singular form arise in the first position in compounds
(for which see Chapter 11), they sometimes retain the -s and they sometimes lose
it, with no apparent logic   though retention of the -s seems more common. Even
individual items may not be consistent. Some examples are given below.

arms control, arms race
card game
checker board, checker-man (US)
clothesline, clothes peg
dart board, darts players
draughts board, draughtsman (Br)
glasses case

goods train (Br)
innings defeat (Br)
mumps epidemic, mumps virus
news broadcast, newspaper
pyjama (US: pajama) top, pyjama (US pajama) trousers
refreshment tent, refreshment trolley, refreshments trolley
scissor blade, scissors grip
staircase, stair-rail
trouser hanger, trouser press

5
THE POSSESSIVE

5.1 Introductory Remarks

The possessive or genitive marker was once part of the inflectional system of English, and in other related languages the corresponding marker is a case marker that occurs on nouns (in some languages, also on adjectives agreeing with nouns in the genitive). In English this is no longer entirely true. Because possession is now shown on the end of a noun phrase, the marker can occur on the ends of words that are not nouns.

Examples:
The man in the iron mask's history.
The man I spoke to's idea.
The woman I met's greeting.
The dog outside's barking is annoying.

In this chapter we will nevertheless give the rules for marking the possessive on nouns. The rules for marking it elsewhere are generally the same, with pronouns being the exception. We deal with those first.

5.2 Possessives on Pronouns

There are two sets of possessive pronouns, the so-called strong and weak forms. The weak possessive pronouns occur before a noun. The strong forms occur in isolation.

Weak possessive pronouns:

> my
> your
> his
> her
> its
> our
> their

There is also an old possessive form for the second person singular, *thy*, which is nowadays used only in religious language (or in some regional dialects) – and even then, increasingly rarely.

The strong possessive pronouns are the following:

> mine
> yours
> his
> hers
> its
> ours
> theirs

Corresponding to *thy*, we have a strong form *thine*, now rarely used.

NOTE ON SPELLING: Note that there is never an apostrophe in the possessive form of pronouns; pronouns can sometimes get an –'s ending when they are at the end of noun phrases as illustrated in Section 5.1 (e.g. *The man who wrote to me's remarks*), but such forms are rare and are not found with possessive pronouns.

5.3   Possessives on Nouns

Rule – spelling:
To mark a noun as possessive, add <'s>. If this results in a sequence of <s's> and the first <s> marks a plural, delete the last <s>.

Rule – sound:
After a regular plural, do not add anything
After a sibilant consonant sound (any of [s, z, ʃ, ʒ, ʧ, ʤ]), add [ɪz].

After any other voiceless consonant sound, add [s].
Everywhere else, add [z].

Examples – spelling:
brother > brother's, brothers > brothers', bus > bus's, cat > cat's, mice > mice's, mouse > mouse's, princess > princess's, women > women's

Examples – sound:
brothers [brʌðəz] > [brʌðəz], cat [kæt] > [kæts], dog [dɒg] > [dɒgz], mouse [maʊs] > [maʊsɪz], owl [aʊl] > [aʊlz], women [wɪmɪn] > [wɪmɪnz]

There is some variation in the spelling following names that end in <s>. Either they can be marked in the spelling with an apostrophe (in which case there is no change in the pronunciation), or they can be marked with -'s (in which case the ending is pronounced /ɪz/). There is a degree of prescriptivism here: foreign names are prescribed to take the simple apostrophe (*Jesus'*, *Sophocles'*) while native names are prescribed to take -'s (*James's*, *Lyons's*). In practice, you might meet either form for either type of name.

ADVICE: Always use the regular (-'s) possessive after names ending in <s>.

POTENTIAL PROBLEM: Because the regular plural form and the regular possessive plural form sound just the same, native speakers of English frequently are confused when writing the forms. The result is that students may come across incorrectly placed apostrophes or omitted apostrophes, especially in unedited texts.

Although the main meaning associated with the possessive is ownership/possession/having, as in *my wife's aunt, the cat's tail, my brother's bike, somebody's bright idea*, it also has a range of other meanings, all of which have in common that they allow a noun phrase to modify a noun. Some examples are given below. While we talk about the possessive form in all of these cases, the meaning is 'possessive' only in a very indirect and general sense.

Agent: John's arrival, the reviewer's criticisms
Classification: a women's magazine, goat's milk, master's degree
Connection with: James Patterson's collaborator, the possessive's function, season's greetings
Location: Hollywood's studios, London's underground system
Named after: Hodgkin's lymphoma, Lou Gehrig's disease

Patient: the prisoner's release, Kennedy's assassination
Purpose: wolf's bane
Time: a summer's day, an hour's work, three weeks' holiday

Note that this means that many expressions with possessives are potentially ambiguous. *Kim's picture* can mean 'the picture Kim owns', 'the picture someone drew/painted/took of Kim', 'the picture Kim drew/painted/took', 'the picture particularly associated with Kim'.

6
COMPARATIVE AND SUPERLATIVE

6.1 Introductory Comments

Both adjectives and adverbs can inflect for degree with comparative and superlative forms. Because the rules in the two cases are not entirely the same, we will treat them separately here.

6.2 Adjectives

6.2.1 The Default

The most usual case for marking comparative and superlative of adjectives is to mark it syntactically, by adding *more* before the adjective to mark the comparative and *most* before the adjective to mark the superlative. This happens nearly all the time with adjectives which are three syllables long or longer, with many two-syllable adjectives, sometimes variably, and sometimes with adjectives of just one syllable.

6.2.2 Irregular Cases

There are a number of adjectives which have irregular comparative and/or superlative forms.

Adjective	Comparative	Superlative	Comment
bad	worse	worst	There is often a regular form used esp. in US slang where *bad* may mean 'attractive'.

Adjective	Comparative	Superlative	Comment
far	farther	farthest	The difference between this and the next is often said to be that *farther* refers to literal distance (*it is farther to York than to London*) but *further* refers to figurative distance (*we will discuss this further*). This is an oversimplification, and *further* is also found for literal distance.
far	further	furthest	
good	better	best	
ill 'in bad health'	worse	—	
old	elder	eldest	Now usually replaced by regular forms, though *elder* is the noun form.
well 'in good health'	better	—	

Although *little* can be used in the comparative and superlative, *smaller* and *smallest* are more common.

6.2.3 The Standard Case

Where the comparative and superlative are not marked by the default method outlined above, they are marked with suffixes.

> **Rule – spelling:**
> Add <er> to the base form of the adjective to mark the comparative, and <est> to mark the superlative.
> Rule S2 changing <y> to <i> before the suffix applies.
> Rule S3 doubling final consonants letters after a stressed short vowel applies.
> Rule S4 deleting a silent <e> before the suffixes applies.

> **Rule – sound:**
> Add [ə] to the base form of the adjective to mark the comparative, [ɪst] to mark the superlative.

In the case of *long* and *strong*, insert [g] between the [ŋ] and the suffix.
Speakers who pronounce words like *simple* with [ə] before the [l], must delete that [ə].

Examples – spelling:
clever > cleverer, cleverest, fine > finer, finest, free > freer [friːə], freest [friːəst], hollow ['hɒləʊ] > hollower, hollowest, pretty > prettier, prettiest, pure > purer, purest, sad > sadder, saddest, thin > thinner, thinnest, weird > weirder, weirdest, zany > zanier, zaniest

Examples – sound:
big [bɪg] > [bɪgə], [bɪgɪst], clever [klevə] > [klevərə], [klevərɪst], pretty [prɪti] > [prɪtiːə], [prɪtiːɪst], rare [reə] > [reərə], [reərɪst], simple [sɪmpl] or [sɪmpəl] > [sɪmplə], [sɪmplɪst], strong [strɒŋ] > [strɒŋgə], [strɒŋgɪst]

ADVICE: It is not possible to give clear and accurate advice on how native English speakers use *-er* and *more* (or *-est* and *most*). Usage is determined by a number of factors, including the phonological structure of the adjective, the morphological structure of the adjective, the syntactic structure in which the comparative is used, the lexical environment in which the construction is used, and even what the recent exposure of the speaker has been to the two constructions. There also appears to be variability between speakers. Accordingly, the best advice we can give is advice which is unlikely to cause problems for native listeners rather than advice which reflects accurately the way that these constructions are used by native speakers.

With words of three or more syllables, always use *more/most* and never *-er/est*: *more expressive, more intelligent, most unusual*.

With monosyllabic adjectives that end in *-st*, use *most* in the superlative: *most moist, most just*.

With monosyllabic adjectives derived from the past participles of verbs, use *more/most*: *more marked, most maimed, most worn*.

With a handful of monosyllabic adjectives always use *more/most*: *fake, like, real, right, wrong*.

With basic adjectives which are monosyllabic and morphologically simple, use *-er/-est* in simple syntactic environments: *the biggest rat I've ever seen, a nicer person would have helped, this one is the smartest, the towel is damper than it should be, November has been wetter than October*.

With two-syllable adjectives which are stressed on the first syllable and end in <y> (though not with the suffix *-ly*), <le>, <ow>, use *-er/-est* in similar syntactic environments: *that's the silliest thing I've ever heard, she has the gentlest voice I know, the river was shallower than I'd expected, a prettier picture.* The two most common adjectives ending in <ow>, *narrow* and *shallow*, are the most likely to take *-er. Yellow* is not often compared, and can go either way.

With two-syllable adjectives that contain suffixes, use *more/most*: *most awesome, more festive, most foolish, more grotesque, most helpful, more likely, most thrilling.* (Strangely, *-er* seems to be counted as an affix, even when it is not, with only *clever* and *slender* preferring *-er* marking, and other words such as *eager, sober* and *tender* preferring to use *more.*)

When comparative or superlative adjectives are coordinated, prefer to use the same construction for both adjectives. This means that if one of the adjectives is trisyllabic or longer, use *more/most* for both; if both can take either construction, use the construction of the first adjective in both positions.

POTENTIAL PROBLEM: For much of the history of English there has been the option of a double comparative, where both the suffix and *more/most* are used. Examples can be found in the works of Shakespeare (*most unkindest cut*), and are regularly heard in spoken English all around the world. Currently this is viewed as being non-standard, and thus should be avoided by learners. However, it is frequent enough that learners who are among native speakers are likely to hear examples of this structure. It appears to mean precisely the same as the single comparative.

POTENTIAL PROBLEM: With an uncountable noun or a plural countable noun, *most* can often be ambiguous between a superlative marker and a quantifier. For example, *most abstruse knowledge* and *the most remote locations* are, at least in writing, ambiguous between 'most knowledge which is abstruse' and 'knowledge which is most abstruse' and 'most of the locations which are remote' and 'the remotest locations', respectively. In speech, the two meanings can be distinguished by phrasing and/or intonation. In practice, it is nearly always clear in context which reading is intended, but care may be required.

6.3   Adverbs

6.3.1   Irregular Cases

There is a set of adverbs with irregular comparative and superlative.

badly	worse	worst
far	farther	farthest
far	further	furthest
little	less	least
much	more	most
well	better	best

6.3.2   The Regular Cases

As with adjectives, there is a suffixed form and a syntactic form. The forms are the same as for the adjectives: *more/most* and *-er/-est*. The rules for the shape of the suffixes are the same as for the suffixes attached to the adjectives. No adverb ending in the suffix *-ly* takes suffixes, they always take *more/most*.

Examples:

early	earlier	earliest
fast	faster	fastest
late	later	latest
soon	sooner	soonest

> POTENTIAL PROBLEM: Just as there is some vacillation in the use of adjective forms for adverbs, there is some variation in the use of comparative and superlative forms. The fixed phrase *That's easier said than done* illustrates an adjectival form where one would expect to find *more easily*.

7
THIRD PERSON SINGULAR -*S*

The suffix -*s* is used to mark the third person singular of what is often called the present tense of verbs which are not modals. A better label for the tense is 'non-past', since these forms can also be used for future time. The modal verbs, which do not show this form, are listed below. Modal verbs use the base form (the unmarked form) in the third person singular of the non-past tense (e.g. *She can help you*). The third person singular means any subject which is, or could be replaced by, any of *he, she,* or *it. The tractor* is third person singular because it can be replaced by *it* in *The tractor/it is pulling a trailer.*

The modal verbs are: *can, could, may, might, must, ought, shall, should, will, would* and, in some constructions, *dare, need, use.*

LEVEL
Although this marking is redundant, omission of it will sound very wrong to native speakers, and it is required from the earliest levels of learning.

7.1 Irregular Forms

There are very few irregular forms here, and they are listed below.

> be + s > is [ɪz]
> do + s > does [dʌz]
> have + s > has [hæz]
> say + s > says [sez]

Says is usually pronounced [sez] (which is what makes it irregular, the spelling is regular), but some speakers regularize it to [seɪz]. This is non-standard, but can be used by learners. The use of [sez] in other persons (*I says*, etc.) is absolutely non-standard, and should be avoided by learners.

7.2   The Regular Case

Rule – spelling:
Add <es> after <s, z, sh, ch, x> and after final <o>.
Otherwise add <s>.
Rule S1 on <y> and <ie> applies.
Rule S3 on consonant letter doubling applies, but has very few opportunities to apply.

Rule – sound:
After a sibilant consonant sound ([s, z, ʃ, ʒ, tʃ, dʒ]), add [ɪz].
After any other voiceless consonant sound, add [s].
Everywhere else, add [z].

Examples – spelling:
arise + s > arises, bus + s > busses, come + s > comes, die + s > dies, enjoy + s > enjoys, fix + s > fixes, go + s > goes, identify + s > identifies, march + s > marches, miss + s > misses, push + s > pushes, quiz + s > quizzes, reply + s > replies, rush + s > rushes, seem + s > seems

Examples – pronunciation:
arise + s > [əˈraɪzɪz], bet + s > [bets], bus + s > [bʌsɪz], come + s > [kʌmz], fall + s > [fɔːlz], fix + s > [fɪksɪz], go + s > [gəʊz], help + s > [helps], laugh + s > [lɑːfs], march + s > [mɑːtʃɪz], push + s > [pʊʃɪz], quiz + s > [kwɪzɪz], reply + s > [rɪˈplaɪz], ski + s > [skiːz], stop + s > [stɒps], work + s > [wɜːks]

8

THE -*ING* FORM OF THE VERB

This is the only really regular piece of morphology in English. The -*ing* can be added to any non-modal verb of English.

LEVEL
Because this is so regular and easy to learn, and because it is so common, it is required from the earliest period of learning.

> **Rule – spelling:**
> **Add -*ing* to the base form of the verb.**
> **Following spelling rule S3, if the base ends in a short vowel followed by a single consonant letter, double the consonant letter.**
> **Following spelling rule S4, if the verb ends in a silent <e>, delete the <e>.**

> **Rule – sound:**
> **Add [ɪŋ] to the base form of the verb.**

Note: The -*ing* form is often pronounced [ɪn] in colloquial usage. Foreign learners should not imitate this usage unless they are extremely fluent.

Examples – spelling:
arrive > arriving, be > being, calm > calming, come > coming, cover > covering, dab > dabbing, do > doing, fill > filling, gas > gassing, revive > reviving, see > seeing, show > showing, sing > singing
Exceptions: busing ~ bussing

Examples – sound:
bus [bʌs] > [ˈbʌsɪŋ], come [kʌm] > [ˈkʌmɪŋ], do [duː] > [ˈduːɪŋ], see [siː] > [ˈsiːɪŋ], sing [sɪŋ] > [ˈsɪŋɪŋ]

The *-ing* form of the verb has several functions (it occurs in the progressive/continuous, it occurs as a non-finite verb form, it occurs as an adjective and as a noun) but the forms are always the same and always regular.

9

PAST TENSE AND PAST PARTICIPLE

9.1   Introduction

The vast majority of verbs are regular. That is, they follow the pattern of *I love*, *I loved*, *I have loved*, or *I wash, I washed, I have washed*. Note that in this pattern the past tense form and the past participle form are identical. There are fewer than 400 verbs which do not follow this regular pattern, but unfortunately, they are often the most common verbs (there are some which used to be common, but no longer are). Here we begin with the regular pattern, and then move on to others, which we term 'irregular' verbs, however that irregularity arises. The classification of irregular verbs is a matter on which grammarians do not agree. Comparing the treatment of irregular verbs in a number of grammars will show a number of different classifications. The classification we provide below has no underlying theoretical principles, but is intended to help the learner.

There is quite a lot of variation in the past tense and past participle forms of verbs. Often, this is a matter of dialect. We use the labels 'US' and 'Br' here as elsewhere to indicate some dialect variation (for more detail, see p. 20). Canadian English often shows variation between the two or a preference for the US form; Australian and New Zealand English are in general more likely to use the British form, though there are individual exceptions. Readers may come across nonstandard, local, idiosyncratic or joke forms of verbs. In general terms, we ignore these since they are rare and may not be predictable.

9.2   The Regular Verbs

Most verbs are regular, and, especially for rare or technical verbs, the regular forms are the most likely. All derived verbs that end in *-ify*, *-ize* and *-en* are regular (e.g.

justify, organize, deafen); all verbs that are formed from nouns or adjectives without any change of form are regular (e.g. *to battle, to empty*); all verbs derived from Latin are regular (e.g. *amalgamate, attract, perceive*); all recent loans are regular (*to boomerang, to tattoo*); all verbs of two or more syllables which do not start with a prefix and are not compounds are regular (e.g. *malinger, speckle*).

Rule – spelling:
If the verb ends in <e>, add <d>; otherwise add *-ed*. If the verb ends in a single consonant which can be doubled by rule S3, double the consonant. If the verb ends in <y>, S2 applies.

Examples:
annoy > annoyed, collapse > collapsed, deny > denied, divide > divided, free > freed, fufil > fulfilled, halo > haloed, laugh > laughed, pin > pinned, pull > pulled, push > pushed, reply > replied, taxi > taxied, try > tried, volley > volleyed, walk > walked

Rule – pronunciation:
If the verb ends in [t] or [d], add [ɪd]; otherwise, if the verb ends in a voiceless consonant, add [t]; in all other cases add [d].

Examples:
dent [dent] > [dentɪd], want [wɒnt] > [wɒntɪd], fade [feɪd] > [feɪdɪd], land [lænd] > [lændɪd], pretend [prɪˈtend] > [prɪˈtendɪd]
hope [həʊp] > [həʊpt], process [ˈprəʊses] > [ˈprəʊsest], push [pʊʃ] > [pʊʃt], feast [fiːst] > [fiːstɪd], walk [wɔːk] > [wɔːkt]
alarm [əˈlɑːm] > [əˈlɑːmd], allow [əˈlaʊ] > [əˈlaʊd], breathe [briːð] > [briːðd], decline [dɪˈklaɪn] > [dɪˈklaɪnd], pull [pʊl] > [pʊld], raise [reɪz] > [reɪzd], try [traɪ] > [traɪd], view [vjuː] > [vjuːd]

POTENTIAL PROBLEM: Where final [t] or [d] follows a consonant, the final consonant cluster may be considerably more difficult for speakers of some languages than a single consonant in this position. Since the loss of the [t] or [d] means the loss of the marking for the past tense or past participle, native speakers find such omissions awkward, except in very fluent speech.

LEVEL
The past tense and past participle forms of regular verbs and the commonest irregular verbs are required from the earliest stages of learning English, and omission of these forms has the potential to cause misunderstanding. Rarer irregular forms are required as the various verbs are introduced. It is implied below that some of

the irregular forms are so rare that they do not need to be taught as part of the active vocabulary, though students may need to recognize them passively.

9.3 Irregular Verbs

9.3.1 Be

The least regular verb is the verb *to be*. It has two past tense forms, basically a singular and a plural. The singular form is *was*, the plural form is *were*. Note that for these purposes, the pronoun *you* counts as plural in English, even when used to address a single person. This strange pattern arises because historically *you* was a plural form, not a singular form. The past participle is *been*.

9.3.2 Verbs which may be Regular or Irregular

There are many verbs which are sometimes regular and sometimes irregular. Sometimes this is a matter of dialect (British English retains some irregularities that tend to vanish elsewhere), sometimes it is just a matter of a certain amount of variation in the system. Relevant verbs are listed below, along with their irregular forms.

Verb	Irregular past tense	Irregular past participle	Comment	Advice
abide	abode	abode		**Avoid; for the sense 'tolerate' use** *stand*; **for the sense 'dwell' use** *live*.
bereave	bereft	bereft	The regular form is most often used in cases of death of a loved one	
beseech	besought	besought		**Avoid, and prefer the regular** *beg*.
bet	bet	bet		
burn	burnt	burnt	The irregular form is Br, the regular form is US	

Verb	Irregular past tense	Irregular past participle	Comment	Advice
bust	bust	bust	The regular form is used in slang to mean 'arrested', while the irregular form is used as an adjective meaning 'bankrupt'	
chide	chid	chid, chidden		**This is now old-fashioned. Use *tell off*.**
cleave	clove, cleft	cloven, cleft	*cleft* and *cloven* are adjectival forms	**Avoid this completely, and use *stick together* or *break apart* as required.**
clothe	clad	clad	*clad* is used adjectivally	
dive	dove	dove	The regular form is Br, the irregular form is US	
drag	drug	drug	The regular form is Br, the irregular form is US or non-standard	
dream	dreamt	dreamt	The irregular form is Br, the regular form is US	
dwell	dwelt	dwelt	The irregular form is Br, the regular form is US	

Verb	Irregular past tense	Irregular past participle	Comment	Advice
fit	fit	fit	The regular form is Br, the irregular form is US	
hang	hung	hung	For some conservative speakers, the regular form is used only for the means of execution. The irregular form is general.	
hew		hewn		**This is poetic, prefer *cut*.**
kneel	knelt	knelt	The regular form is particularly used in the US	
knit	knit	knit	The difference between the two forms may be semantic, with *knitted* used of bones and brows and *knit* used of making things with wool	
lean	leant	leant	The irregular form is mainly Br	
leap	leapt	leapt	The regular form is mainly US	

Verb	Irregular past tense	Irregular past participle	Comment	Advice
learn	learnt	learnt	The irregular form is Br, the regular form is US; the adjectival form is [lɜːnɪd]	
light	lit	lit		
mow		mown		
plead	pled	pled	The irregular form is mainly US	
prove		proven	*Proven*, which may be [pruːvən] or [prəʊvən], is often adjectival or Scottish or US	
quit	quit	quit	The regular form is mainly Br	
rid	rid	rid	*Ridded* is rare	**Alternatives such as *free* or *remove from* are usually preferable.**
saw		sawn		
sew		sewn		
shave		shaven	*Shaven* is mostly the adjectival form	
shear	shore	shorn		
shine	shone	shone ([ʃɒn] is Br, [ʃəʊn] is US)	The transitive verb is usually regular	
shit	shat, shit	shat, shit		**Avoid because it is rude. In medical contexts use *have a motion*.**

Verb	Irregular past tense	Irregular past participle	Comment	Advice
shoe	shod	shod		
show		shown	The irregular past participle is the more usual one	
shred	shred	shred	The regular form is usual	
shrive	shrove	shriven		**Use *forgive* or *pardon* where possible.**
smell	smelt	smelt	The irregular form is Br, the regular form is US	
sneak	snuck	snuck	The regular form is Br, the irregular form is US or informal	
sow		sown		
speed	sped	sped		
spell	spelt	spelt	The irregular form is Br, the regular form is US	
spill	spilt	spilt	The irregular form is Br, the regular form is US	
spoil	spoilt	spoilt	The irregular form is Br, the regular form is US	
stove	stove	stove		**Rare in all meanings, avoid.**
strew		strewn		**Poetic in style, use *scatter*.**
strive	strove	striven		**Formal, prefer *try*.**

Verb	Irregular past tense	Irregular past participle	Comment	Advice
sweat	sweat	sweat	Although the irregular form is sometimes prescribed, the regular form is more usual	**In a literal sense,** *perspire* **is a regular alternative.**
swell		swollen	The irregular form is probably more usual	
thrive	throve	thriven	The irregular past participle in particular is old-fashioned	*Prosper* **and** *flourish* **are regular verbs which can be substituted for this rather literary word.**
tread	trod, tread	trodden, tread	The regular form is rare; the form *tread* is mainly US, but not common there	
wake	woke	woken	The regular form of *wake* is rare, but is normal with *awake*	
weave	wove	woven	The irregular form is used for making cloth, the regular form is most often used for running between obstacles	

Verb	Irregular past tense	Irregular past participle	Comment	Advice
wed	wed	wed	The adjectival form is *wedded*	**In active use, prefer the regular *marry*.**
wet	wet	wet		

ADVICE: Except for *hang*, which may be used in the irregular form in all meanings, the regular forms of these verbs may be used. The irregular forms need to be recognized at intermediate levels or above. Note that the regular forms are particularly suitable with the rarest verbs, which has benefits in the teaching situation. Some of these verbs can be avoided completely. *Shit* is usually best avoided in polite society; *wed* is found mostly in newspaper headlines, and *marry* is preferred; *hew* may be replaced with *cut*; *cleave* is the amalgam of two verbs with opposite meanings, and is best avoided except in fixed phrases.

9.3.3   Verbs with only One Form

A number of verbs that are monosyllabic and end in <t> or <d> have only a single form, with the base being the same as the past tense and the past participle. These verbs are listed below. Note that if they take prefixes, they retain this form.

> bet, bust, cast (also broadcast, forecast, etc.), cost, cut (also undercut etc.), fit (US; also refit), hit, hurt, knit (US), let (both meaning 'allow' and meaning 'hire out'), put (also input, output, etc.), quit, read (in spelling only, the past tense and past participle forms are [red]; also proofread, reread, etc.), rid, set (also preset, reset, upset, etc.), shed, shit (variable), shred, shut, slit, spit (US), sweat, text (only from young people), thrust, tread (with much variation), wed, wet

9.3.4   Some High Frequency Idiosyncratic Forms

Some high frequency verbs have idiosyncratic patterns which are either unique or have very few members. Some such verbs are listed below. Some of these have other patterns in dialectal or non-standard usage, but these alternatives are not considered here, even though they may be common in speech.

Base form	Past tense	Past participle	Comment
break	broke	broken	
come	came	come	Also become, overcome
do	did	done	Also outdo, undo, etc.
draw	drew	drawn	
eat	ate [et] or [eɪt]	eaten	
fall	fell	fallen	Also befall
give	gave	given	Also forgive
go	went	gone	Also forego, undergo
have	had	had	
lose	lost	lost	
make	made	made	Also remake etc.
say	said [sed]	said [sed]	Also gainsay
see	saw	seen	Also foresee
sell	sold	sold	Also outsell etc.
stand	stood	stood	Also understand etc.
tell	told	told	Also foretell etc.

The verb *get* has the past tense form *got* and the past participle is *got* in Br but there is a semantically distinct past participle *gotten* in US. *Gotten* cannot be used when the meaning is 'have', as in *He has got enough food*. Ironically, given that *forget* is originally a derivative of *get*, the Br usage is to have *forgot* as the past tense and *forgotten* as the past participle, while the US usage is to have *forgot* for both. *Beget* always has *begot, begotten*.

9.3.5 Ablaut A

Ablaut is vowel change which is not historically determined by another vowel in the word. In present-day English the difference between umlaut and ablaut is not visible, though the terminology is standard. In this first pattern of ablaut, the past tense has the vowel sound [æ] and the past participle has the vowel sound [ʌ]. Most of the verbs have a base form with the vowel sound [ɪ], but there are a few marginal examples with a different vowel. The relevant verbs are set out below.

Base form	Past tense	Past participle	Comment
begin	began	begun	
drink	drank	drunk	
sing	sang	sung	
sink	sank	sunk	
swim	swam	swum	
run	ran	run	also outrun, overrun, etc.

For further discussion of this pattern, see the comparison in the discussion of Ablaut B in Section 9.3.6.

9.3.6 Ablaut B

In this pattern of ablaut, both the past tense and the past participle have the vowel sound [ʌ]. Most of the verbs have a base form with the vowel sound [ɪ], but there are a few marginal examples with a different vowel. The relevant verbs are set out below.

Base form	Past tense	Past participle	Comment
cling	clung	clung	
fling	flung	flung	
sling	slung	slung	
slink	slunk	slunk	
stick	stuck	stuck	
sting	stung	stung	
string	strung	strung	Also hamstring, restring, etc.
swing	swung	swung	
win	won [wʌn]	won [wʌn]	
wring	wrung	wrung	
drag	drug	drug	This is US, Br has a regular verb here
hang	hung	hung	Also overhang, rehang, etc.
sneak	snuck	snuck	This is US, Br has a regular verb here

There is competition between the patterns in Ablaut A and Ablaut B. In both cases, the base forms usually have the vowel sound [ɪ] followed by a velar consonant or consonants: <ck>, <g>, <ng>, <nk> ([k], [g], [ŋ]). *Shrink* can take either pattern. The verbs *run* and *win* end in a non-velar nasal, which is unusual for this pattern. The pattern in Ablaut B covers more verbs.

> ADVICE: Advanced learners may become aware of hearing the Ablaut B pattern on verbs which are expected to take the Ablaut A pattern. Such usage is non-standard, but widespread. This means that if the learner is in doubt, it is safer to use the pattern in Ablaut B. Note that for the past participle, it will make no difference which of these is used.

9.3.7 Ablaut C

In this pattern the base form has the vowel sound [iː], and the past tense and past participle both have the vowel sound [e]. All these verbs end in <t> or <d> in the past tense and past participle. Sometimes this means that a final <t> or <d> is added in these forms as well as the vowel change. The relevant verbs are presented below.

Base form	Past tense	Past participle	Comment
bleed	bled	bled	
breed	bred	bred	Also crossbreed, inbreed, interbreed, etc.
cleave	cleft	cleft	Note the extra final <t>; this verb can be used with a regular pattern or replaced with a more common verb
deal	dealt	dealt	Note the extra final <t>; also misdeal, redeal
dream	dreamt	dreamt	Note the extra final <t>; this is Br, US has a regular verb
feed	fed	fed	Also handfeed, overfeed, spoonfeed, etc.
feel	felt	felt	Note the extra final <t>
flee	fled	fled	Note the extra final <d>
keep	kept	kept	Note the extra final <t>
kneel	knelt	knelt	Note the extra final <t>
lead	led	led	Also mislead. Note the spelling: *lead* can also spell [led], the metal
lean	leant	leant	Note the extra final <t>; this form is Br, US has a regular verb
leap	leapt	leapt	Note the extra final <t>; US has a regular verb
leave	left	left	Note the extra final <t>, which changes the <v> into an <f>
mean	meant	meant	Note the extra final <t>
meet	met	met	
plead	pled	pled	This form is mainly US; a regular form is also used
read [riːd]	read [red]	read [red]	Note that in terms of spelling this is a single-form verb, but in terms of its pronunciation, it fits here; also misread, proofread, reread, etc.
sleep	slept	slept	Note the extra final <t>; also oversleep, etc.
speed	sped	sped	This verb is also used regularly

9.3.8   Ablaut D

There are various patterns and sub-patterns of ablaut which affect verbs whose vowel sound in the base form is [aɪ].

In the first pattern, the base form has the vowel sound [aɪ] and the past tense has the vowel sound [əʊ]; the past participle is either like the past tense (sub-pattern (a)) or has the vowel sound [ɪ] and the suffix -*en* (sub-pattern (b)). Sub-pattern (b) is the more common pattern. The relevant verbs are presented below.

Base form	Past tense	Past participle	Comment	Advice
abide	abode	abode	(a) This form is found only when *abide* means 'stay, live'; *abide* meaning 'like' is regular	**Use *live* or *like* rather than *abide*.**
dive	dove	dove	(a) This form is mainly US; the regular form is also used	
drive	drove	driven	(b)	
ride	rode	ridden	(b); also override, etc.	
rise	rose	risen	(b); also arise	
shine	shone	shone	(a); this verb fits this pattern only in US; in Br, the past tense and past participle are pronounced [ʃɒn]; the verb is also used regularly, especially in transitive uses	
shrive	shrove	shriven	(b); also used regularly	**This is used only for a ceremony in some of the Christian churches, and is correspondingly rare.**

Base form	Past tense	Past participle	Comment	Advice
smite	smote	smitten	(b)	**This is old-fashioned or poetic, and can always be avoided. In various meanings** *strike, overcome, be affected by* **and, in the past participle,** *in love* **can be used.**
stride	strode		Speakers are unsure of the past participle form and tend to avoid it; both pattern (a) and pattern (b) are found, as is the regular form	**Use** *take strides* **or the like to avoid the issue.**
strive	strove	striven	(b); also used regularly	**Use** *try* **instead.**
thrive	throve	thriven	(b); also used regularly	**Use** *flourish* **or** *prosper,* **both of which are regular.**
write	wrote	written	(b); also handwrite, rewrite, underwrite, etc.	

The next pattern has the vowel sound [aɪ] in the base form, and the vowel sound [aʊ] in the past tense and past participle. The relevant verbs are listed below.

Base form	Past tense	Past participle	Comment
bind	bound	bound	Also unbind
find	found	found	
grind	ground	ground	Also regrind
wind	wound	wound	Also overwind, rewind, etc.

In the next set the past tense always has the vowel sound [ɪ], but the past participle sometimes has the suffix -*en* (pattern (a)) and sometimes is just the same as the past tense (pattern (b)). Some verbs vary between these patterns.

Base form	Past tense	Past participle	Comment	Advice
bite	bit	bitten	(a) The past participle *bit* is US	
chide	chid	chidden	(a) Also regular	**This is literary; avoid and use *tell off* instead.**
hide	hid	hidden	(a) The past participle *hid* is US	
light	lit	lit	(b) Also regular; also moonlight, relight, etc.	
slide	slid	slid	(b) Also backslide	

Finally, there is a small set of verbs which do not fit in any generalizable pattern. *Strike* might be considered an irregular member of pattern Ablaut B.

Base form	Past tense	Past participle	Comment
fly	flew	flown	
lie	lay	lain	Also underlie
strike	struck	struck	There is an adjectival form *stricken*

9.3.9   Ablaut E

In this pattern, the base form of the verb contains the vowel sound [əʊ] and the past tense either contains the vowel sound [uː] (pattern (a)) or has a regular past tense (pattern (b)). The past participle has [əʊ] but with an *-en* suffix. The relevant verbs are listed below.

Base form	Past tense	Past participle	Comment
blow	blew	blown	(a)
grow	grew	grown	(a); also regrow, outgrow
know	knew	known	(a)
mow		mown	(b); also regular
sew		sewn	(b); also resew, oversew, etc.
show		shown	(b)
sow		sown	(b)
throw	threw	thrown	(a); also overthrow, etc.

9.3.10   Ablaut F

In this pattern the base form has the vowel sound [eə] and the past tense and past participle have the vowel sound [ɔː]. The past participle has the suffix -n. The relevant verbs are listed below.

Base form	Past tense	Past participle	Comment
bear	bore	borne	Note the regular spelling <born> in relation to birth; also forebear, etc.
swear	swore	sworn	Also forswear
tear	tore	torn	
wear	wore	worn	

9.3.11   Ablaut G

In this pattern, the base form has the vowel sound [iː], the past tense has the vowel sound [əʊ], and the past participle has the vowel sound [əʊ] and a final -en.

Base form	Past tense	Past participle	Comment	Advice
cleave	clove	cloven	This verb is more usually used in the regular form, though *cloven* is an adjectival form in some fixed expressions	**Avoid this, and use *stick to* or *part from* as appropriate.**
freeze	froze	frozen		
heave	hove	hove	This verb is used only in the expression *heave into sight*, used of ships; all other uses of *heave* are regular	**Avoid, and use *come into sight* if required.**
speak	spoke	spoken	Also misspeak, etc.	
steal	stole	stolen		
weave	wove	woven	Also interweave, etc.	

9.3.12 *Ablaut H*

The patterns presented here are minor patterns, probably best viewed as exceptions to the other rules. Verbs showing parallel patterns have been put together in the following list.

Base form	Past tense	Past participle	Comment	Advice
bid	bade [bæd] or [beɪd]	bidden	This verb means 'request'; the verb for 'enter an offer at an auction' has a different pattern; also forbid	**This is old-fashioned; use *ask* or *tell* instead.**
blow	blew	blown		
grow	grew	grown	Also outgrow, etc.	
know	knew	known		
throw	threw	thrown	Also overthrow, etc.	
choose	chose	chosen		
clothe	clad	clad	Also regular	**You can always use the verb *dress* instead.**
dig	dug	dug		
draw	drew	drawn	Also outdraw, withdraw, etc.	
forsake	forsook	forsaken		**There are many words that can be used to replace this literary word, including *abandon* and *jilt*.**
shake	shook	shaken		
take	took	taken	Also mistake	
wake	woke	woken	Also awaken	
hear	heard	heard	Also mishear, overhear, etc.	
hew		hewn	Also regular	**Poetical, avoid and use *cut*.**
hold	held	held	Also withhold, etc.	

Base form	Past tense	Past participle	Comment	Advice
lose	lost	lost		
shave		shaven	Also regular	
show		shown		
shoe	shod	shod	Also regular	

9.3.13 Verbs with Past Tense and Past Participle in [ɔːt]

A number of verbs with rather different base forms share past tense and past participle forms in [ɔːt], usually spelt <ought>, sometimes spelt <aught>. The verbs
are listed below.

Base form	Past tense	Past participle	Comment
beseech	besought	besought	
buy	bought	bought	
bring	brought	brought	The irregular forms of *buy* and *bring* are often confused by native speakers
catch	caught	caught	
fight	fought	fought	Also outfight
seek	sought	sought	
teach	taught	taught	Also reteach, etc.
think	thought	thought	Also overthink, etc.

9.3.14 Verbs with Irregular [t]

Some past tense and past participle forms end with an unexpected [t], either as an
affix or as a replacement for the [d] at the end of the base form. Where the base
form contains the vowel sound [iː], these have been dealt with under Ablaut C, but
are repeated here. Relevant verbs are listed below.

Base form	Past tense	Past participle	Comment	Advice
bend	bent	bent	Also unbend	
build	built	built	Also rebuild, etc.	
burn	burnt	burnt	This form is Br, the regular form is US	
deal	dealt [delt]	dealt [delt]	Also redeal, etc.; see Ablaut C	
dream	dreamt [dremt]	dreamt [dremt]	Also daydream; see Ablaut C; this form is Br, the regular form is US	

Base form	Past tense	Past participle	Comment	Advice
dwell	dwelt	dwelt		
feel	felt	felt	See Ablaut C	
keep	kept [kept]	kept [kept]	See Ablaut C	
leap	leapt [lept]	leapt [lept]	See Ablaut C	
learn	learnt	learnt	This form is Br, the regular form is US; also relearn, etc.	
lend	lent	lent		
rend	rent	rent		**Avoid and use *tear* instead.**
send	sent	sent	Also resend	
sleep	slept	slept	See Ablaut C; also oversleep, etc.	
smell	smelt	smelt	This form is Br; the regular form is US	
spend	spent	spent		
spell	spelt	spelt	This form is Br; the regular form is US	
spill	spilt	spilt	This form is Br; the regular form is US	
spoil	spoilt	spoilt	This form is Br; the regular form is US	
sweep	swept [swept]	swept [swept]	See Ablaut C	
weep	wept [wept]	wept [wept]	See Ablaut C	

ADVICE: Learn the high frequency idiosyncratic verbs and the Ablaut A verbs. Once you have learnt these in all three forms, for other verbs learn the base and the past participle. Unless the past participle ends in -*n*, assume that the past tense form is the same as the past participle.

10
NUMBERS

10.1   The Basic Numbers

The basic numbers in English are given below.

1	one
2	two
3	three
4	four
5	five
6	six
7	seven
8	eight
9	nine
10	ten
11	eleven
12	twelve
100	hundred
1,000	thousand
1,000,000	million

10.2   13–19

The numbers in the range 13–19 have the suffix -*teen*. The numbers 13 and 15 have irregular forms of the base: *thirteen, fifteen*. In the name for number 18, there is only one <t> (and for most speakers only one [t]) in the word.

10.3 20–90

The numbers from 20 to 90 have the suffix *-ty*. The names for 20, 30, 40 and 50 have irregular forms, the name for 80 has only one <t> (and only one [t]).

20 twenty
30 thirty
40 forty
50 fifty
60 sixty
70 seventy
80 eighty
90 ninety

Note that although *forty* has an irregular spelling, its pronunciation is perfectly regular in southern British English, although there are varieties of English where the pronunciation is also irregular.

Intermediate numbers between 20 and 30 (and so on) are made up of the number of tens (e.g. *twenty*) and the appropriate basic number (up to 9), e.g. *twenty-five*, *thirty-nine*, *sixty-seven* and so on.

Larger numbers can be made on the patterns below.

Three hundred and seventy-six (376)
Five thousand, two hundred and seven (5,207)
Nine thousand and ninety-nine (9,099)
Five million, three hundred and nine thousand, seven hundred and nineteen (5,309,719)
Two hundred and twenty-nine million and six (229,000,006)

POTENTIAL PROBLEMS: In US English, the word *and* is omitted in structures like *three hundred and twenty-one*.

Three-digit numbers can also be read without the *hundred and*, so that 237 becomes *two thirty-seven* and 509 becomes *five oh nine*. Note the use of *oh* [əʊ]. The distribution of *oh* and *zero* and *nought* for 0 is not entirely agreed.

Four-digit numbers are often split into two, so that 5,981 can be read as *fifty-nine eighty-one*. This method is common in reading years in dates: 1066 *ten sixty-six*, 1604 *sixteen oh four*, 2018 *twenty eighteen*. This reading style is also used with currency, so that $49·50 is read as *forty-nine fifty* and $562·95 is read as *five sixty-two ninety-five*.

In principle, larger numbers follow the same patterns as those just illustrated, but in practice any number larger than a million (used virtually exclusively in science and economics) is given as a round number or with a decimal point following it (e.g. *2·5 trillion*). The larger numbers are not given here.

The word *billion* is now usually used to mean 1,000,000,000, though in British English it used to mean (and sometimes still does) 1,000,000,000,000.

100, 1,000, 1,000,000 can be said as *one hundred, one thousand, one million* or as *a hundred, a thousand, a million*. The form with the indefinite article is less likely in long numbers such as 1,109,155, and most likely when the relevant form is initial in the number being pronounced.

Because *-ty* and *-teen* can sound very similar when said quickly, it is quite usual to hear questions like '1–8 or 8–0?' (with the 0 pronounced *oh*), and equally common to hear numbers clarified in this way.

Note the use of the commas to split up numbers larger than 999, and the use of the decimal point '·' (and not a comma) to show tenths of one unit.

Numbers after the decimal point are pronounced individually: 3·225 is pronounced as *three point two two five* (and not as **point two hundred and twenty-five*).

10.4 Ordinal Numbers

The fundamental rule for the creation of ordinal numbers from cardinal numbers is to add *-th* [θ]. There are many irregularities, though.

1	first
2	second
3	third
5	fifth

All the words ending in *-ty* have an ordinal form in *-ieth* (*twentieth, sixtieth* and so on), following spelling rule S2.

Fractions also have the same *-th* on the end, so that ⅙ is *one sixth*. However, there are again some irregularities.

½	a half
⅓	a third
¼	a quarter
⅕	a fifth

10.5 Distributive Numbers

There are various types of distributive numbers in English. The obvious one is to use an apparent plural marker: *in twos, in tens, in thirties, in hundreds*.

We also find the number in an expression *X at a time*, as in: *two at a time, ten at a time, thirty at a time, a hundred at a time*. An equivalent expression is illustrated by *two-by-two*, but this construction is not often used with numbers over ten.

The term *singly* can also be used in the same way as *one at a time*, but *doubly* and *triply* are multipliers, like words ending in *-fold*.

The suffix *-fold* is relatively formal and rare. It means 'multiplied by ~' so that *a five-fold increase* is an increase by a factor of five: *twofold, ten-fold, thirty-fold, hundredfold*.

Such forms can be used as adjectives or adverbs, so both *a five-fold increase* and *Their profit increased five-fold* are possible.

10.6 Oddities

There is a number *ump* which never occurs in that form, but only in forms such as *umpteen, umpty-ump(th)*. *Ump* is some unidentified relatively large number. *Umpteen* is used to be vague about a number (*There were umpteen people trying to catch the waiter's eye*), *umpty-umpth* is typically used to avoid stating an age (*It was his umpty-umpth birthday*). The figure *a hundred and one* is sometimes used in a similar way for an indefinite large number (e.g. *I've told you a hundred and one times not to do that*).

There is a series of joke numbers for extremely large but imprecise numbers: *zillion, gazillion, bajillion, squillion*, etc. There is a lot of variation in the initial letters of this construction.

For prefixes which create numbers, see Section 16.4.

11
COMPOUNDS

11.1 Introduction

A compound is a word whose elements are also words. English has a large number of compounds of many types. Speakers of other European languages will find many types which are familiar to them. More difficult to deal with are the types which do not exist or are unusual in English, but are common in other languages. Types in which two elements are equivalent (e.g. *hot-sour*, *murder-suicide*) are far more common in Asian languages than in English. Types in which a verb and a noun together create an agent noun (e.g. *dreadnaught*, *spoilsport*) are common in Romance languages, and very rare in English.

In general terms, there are only two types which are so common that they can be used and invented by learners. The first of these types is a noun made up of a verb, a noun and an affix. These are given many names in the literature (e.g. 'synthetic compounds', 'verb-centred compounds'), we will term them 'verbal nexus compounds'. The second type is the type where two nouns go together to form a new noun. These are called 'endocentric compounds'. These two types will be dealt with in turn below.

11.2 Verbal-nexus Compounds

Verbal-nexus compounds are compounds like *taxi-driver*, *taxi-driving*. In this type of compound we have a verb (*drive* in the examples above), the direct object of that verb (*taxi* in the examples above: somebody drives the taxi), and a suffix *-er* or *-ing*. A *taxi-driver* is a person who drives a taxi (if machines could drive taxis, *taxi-driver* could also denote such a machine), *taxi-driving* is the profession or skill of being able to drive a taxi.

This pattern is freely available. If you saw someone chasing a dog, you could ask whether dog-chasing is a sport or whether the dog-chaser is enjoying the task, even though nobody has ever heard the words *dog-chaser* or *dog-chasing* before. They are easily understandable.

Some examples of this pattern that are well-established in English are given below. A distinction is drawn here between compounds which denote people, compounds which denote animals and compounds which denote machines or things, but the pattern applies equally to all three types without distinction. Note that the spelling of these compounds is not entirely consistent, but that stress is regularly on the direct object.

People	*Animals*	*Machines/Things*
asylum seeker	anteater	dish-washer
bread-winner	bee-eater	egg-beater
bus-driver	flycatcher	ice-breaker
dressmaker	goat-sucker	pipe-cleaner
landowner	woodpecker	tea-strainer
lion-hunter		water-cooler
metalworker		wind-cheater ('type of
mind reader		jacket')
snake-charmer		
sun-worshipper		

The pattern with *-ing* is illustrated below with some well-established examples. The stress here is not entirely predictable.

city planning
lip-reading
mischief-making
money-making
profit-sharing
sheep-shearing
shipbuilding

The second element *-monger* appears only in constructions like these, and means 'a person who sells ~' (sometimes the selling is figurative). This is used only in a few words, now rather old-fashioned, and you should not invent new words on this pattern. The most frequent relevant examples are

fishmonger 'a person who sells fish'
gossip-monger 'a person who passes on gossip'
ironmonger (Br) 'a person who sells nails, tools, etc.'

newsmonger 'a person who sells newspapers and magazines'
warmonger 'a person who encourages violent policies'

Although the pattern with -*er* and -*ing* and the direct object of the verb is the only pattern you should feel free to use yourself, you need to recognize that there are other similar patterns which have a slightly different interpretation or form. You need to be aware of these patterns to interpret them, but you should only use words of this type if you have heard them. Stress in these patterns is less predictable.

(a) The initial noun is not the direct object of the verb, but indicates the location of the action of the verb. Examples: *bellylanding, cave-dweller, garden-warbler, sea-bathing, sky-writing, strip mining, town crier, tree creeper*

(b) The initial noun is not the direct object of the verb, but indicates the time at which the action takes place. Examples: *daydreaming, nightwalker, sleep-walking, spring cleaning, summer visitor, Sunday driver*

(c) The initial noun is not the direct object of the verb, but in a syntactic paraphrase requires a preposition. Examples: *baby-sitting* (sits with or for a baby), *glass-maker* (makes things of glass), *horse whisperer* (whispers to horses), *housebreaker* (breaks into houses), *lead poisoning* (poisons with lead), *movie goer* (goes to movies), *peace worker* (works for peace), *precision bombing* (bombs with precision), *pressure-cooker* (cooks with/using pressure), *prison escaper* (escapes from prison), *prize fighter* (fights for a prize)

(d) The initial noun is not the direct object of the verb, but denotes something that the second element also is or resembles. Examples: *cub reporter, jet fighter, learner driver, peasant farmer*

(e) The initial noun is not the direct object of the verb, but something possessed. Examples: *cabin cruiser, motor scooter*

(f) The initial noun is not the direct object of the verb, but the subject. Example: *government hiring*

(g) Instead of ending in -*ing*, the rightmost word is a noun derived from a verb in some other way. The initial noun is still the direct object of the verb. Provided you know the appropriate form of the noun, forms on this pattern can still be invented. Examples: *air pollution, bill payment, garbage disposal, population control, student assessment, verb conjugation*

(h) The initial noun is in the same relationships as shown in (a)–(f), but the form is as shown in (g). You should recognize these patterns, but only use examples you have heard. Examples: *heart failure, police protection, satellite communication, tax concession*

11.3 Endocentric Compounds

In endocentric noun compounds there are two nouns side-by-side. The compound as a whole denotes a subtype of the righthand noun (which is sometimes called the 'head' noun). For example, a *textbook* is a type of book, and *book* is the head noun, a *windmill* is a type of mill, and *mill* is the head noun. Because at least some of the compounds with nouns created from verbs belong in the verbal-nexus compounds, it is safest to assume that the set involved here does not involve such head nouns.

Stress in such constructions is variable, as is the spelling. Where the stress is concerned, the safest way to predict is to assume that a new compound will have the same stress as another compound with the same head noun. This is not always true, but is usually true. For example, *banana cake, carrot cake, cattle cake, cheese-cake, chocolate cake, Christmas cake, coffee cake, fish cake, oatcake* all have stress on the first noun, while *apple pie, cherry pie, custard pie, (h)umble pie, plum pie, pork pie* have stress on the head noun (but *potpie* has stress on the first noun). While stress is not predictable from the spelling for endocentric compounds written with a hyphen or as two distinct words, endocentric compounds that are written as one word (like *potpie*) almost always have initial stress, and of those that do not, most have a variant with initial stress. However, it must be underlined that this is a generalization over endocentric compounds which (a) are not names/proper nouns, (b) have a noun in both elements, (c) act as nouns in the sentence. Although the generalization may look as though it is true over a larger number of compounds, there are many exceptions which break any one of these conditions.

In general terms it is safe to invent new endocentric compound nouns. For example, although I have never (to my knowledge) heard the expression *psychology dividend*, if you were talking about the benefits of higher education, and you said that you felt that you now understood people better, and added *That's probably my psychology dividend*, I would understand that you meant that having studied psychology was rewarding you. Endocentric compounds of this type are generally easy to understand in context, but may not work out of context, especially if there is an existing word for the relevant item which is different from the word you have made up.

ADVICE: Although many endocentric compounds ending in *-man* exist, you should avoid inventing any. This is for both formal and social reasons. Formally, many, but not all, such compounds have an unpredictable *-s-* before the *man* (*groundsman, swordsman, tradesman*); also the stress on the *-man* element is not always predictable, so that sometimes we find [mæn] and sometimes [mən]. Socially, compounds in *man* once denoted either men or women, but now they are perceived as applying to men only, and are considered sexist terms. Many words with *-man* are now replaced with other terms: *fireman* becomes *fire fighter*, *policeman* becomes *police officer*, *seaman* becomes *seafarer* and so on. There are always other ways of creating nouns which denote agents.

11.4   Other Types of Compound

Although you should not invent any other types of compound without quite a lot of experience to back you up, you will find many. Compounds can be found in all word-classes, as shown below.

Modifying element	Head				
	Noun	Adjective	Verb	Adverb	Preposition
Noun	police officer	sky-blue, word-final	colour-code	word-finally	year in, year out
Adjective	whiteboard	dark-green, deaf-mute	fine-tune		due to
Verb	crybaby	fail safe	stir-fry		
Adverb	now generation		outachieve		apart from
Preposition	downdraught	uptight	upgrade		into

Compounds can also be found where the word-class of the compound is not the same as the word-class of the head of the compound. Learners should not attempt to create such words, but will need to recognize them from time to time. Some examples are given below. Such compounds are called exocentric compounds.

Head is	Compound acts as			
	Noun	Verb	Adjective	Adverb
Noun		breath-test, brown-bag, test-market	two-syllable, back-street	flat-stick
Verb	nose-bleed, input, make-believe		pass-fail, quick-change, stop-go, tow-away	
Adjective				double-quick

12

MAKING NOUNS

Because English is rich in ways in which to make nouns, there are multiple intersecting classes. There are nouns made from verbs, there are nouns denoting people, there are nouns whose meaning is transparent and others whose meaning has to be learnt. Because of this complexity, there is no ideal way to present the material. Here, in line with what is done elsewhere in this book, we classify nouns on the basis of what kind of base they are attached to. Where possible, affixes which mean similar things are treated close together, but this does not always make sense in terms of other factors such as how useful a particular affix is for the learner. To find nouns with particular meanings, consult the index.

12.1   Nouns from other Nouns

12.1.1   The Suffix -dom

The suffix -*dom* makes three main types of nouns. The first is those meaning 'an area ruled by a ~' (where the swung dash shows the word in the base). For instance, a *kingdom* is an area ruled by a king. The second is those meaning 'the collection of all entities denoted by the base'. For instance, *poodledom* is the collection of all poodles. The third is those meaning 'the quality of being a ~ or the state of being a ~'. For instance, *serfdom* is the quality of being a serf. Sometimes it is not easy to distinguish these three meanings: poodledom might be ruled by a poodle, and show the quality of being a poodle. An earl might rule over an earldom, or be elevated to an earldom, to the status of being an earl. The suffix -*dom* is usually added to words denoting people or animals, but sometimes it is extended. The word *poodledom* also shows that some recent words made with this suffix are intended to be humorous rather than serious. Although people can make new words in this way, it is safer to use those you have already heard.

Examples 1 – area ruled:
earl + -dom > earldom
heathen + -dom > heathendom
king + -dom > kingdom
peer +-dom > peerdom
prince + -dom > princedom
tsar + -dom > tsardom

Examples 2 – collection of entities:
monk + -dom > monkdom
scoundrel + -dom > scoundreldom
student + -dom > studentdom

Examples 3 – state or quality:
fool + -dom > fooldom
martyr + -dom > martyrdom
thrall + -dom > thralldom

12.1.2 The Suffixes -hood and -ship

The suffix *-hood* makes nouns meaning 'the state of being a ~'. For example, *motherhood* is the state of being a mother. Unlike *-dom*, *-hood* is regularly found with non-person nouns in the base: *wordhood* is the state of being a word.

Examples:
child + -hood > childhood
mother + -hood > motherhood
state + -hood > statehood

Nouns ending in *-hood* can also mean 'the period during which one is a ~', so that *childhood* can mean 'the period during which one is a child'. *Manhood* can mean 'the qualities a man is supposed to have' and *brotherhood* can mean 'a group of men with a common purpose', as well as having the expected readings.

The suffix *-ship*, like *-hood*, makes words meaning 'the state of being ~', but there are often other meanings attached to this suffix.

Examples:
champion + -ship > championship (also 'contest to determine a champion')
friend + -ship > friendship (also 'mutual liking')
leader + -ship > leadership
musician + -ship > musicianship ('the skill or art of a musician')

Sometimes, *-ship* indicates a title: *ladyship, lordship*. It is also occasionally used to indicate jobs (*headmastership, tutorship*), and in some words its meaning is difficult to discern: *township* ('small town, area of a town, administrative area'), *courtship* ('the time over which a person is wooed prior to a proposal of marriage').

12.1.3 Marking Locations

Two affixes are used to make locational nouns from other nouns, but in neither case is it the primary usage of the affix. You should not use either of these patterns to invent new words.

The suffix *-age* has a number of meanings, of which location is just one. Locational nouns with *-age* include *hermitage, orphanage, parsonage*.

The suffix *-ery* also has a number of meanings, though rather different from those of *-age*. Locational nouns with *-ery* include *cannery, creamery, fernery, joinery, nunnery, nursery, piggery, rockery, rookery, shrubbery, swannery, winery*.

LEVEL
Individual words with these patterns are common (*bakery, butchery, vicarage*), but because this use of *-age* is relatively rare, the location meaning can be ignored until other uses have been met.

12.1.4 Marking Collections

The same two suffixes can also mark collections of items. Again, this is not the principal meaning of *-age*, but it probably is one of the principal meanings of *-ery*. We have already seen a similar usage of *-dom*. The suffix *-iana* (sometimes *-ana* or *-na*) can be used, mostly on the names of famous people, to denote collections of things associated with the noun in the base. Examples of all three are given below. Again, you should probably not use these to invent new words. The phonology of *-iana* is awkward. The <i> seems to be present only when there is an *-ian* adjective on the same base; the suffix takes the stress, and if there is an <o> preceding the suffix it is pronounced [əʊ] (e.g. [nɪksəʊniˈɑːnə]).

-age: coinage, herbage, signage, plumage, sewerage, wordage
-ery: confectionery, crockery, cutlery, jewellery, machinery, pottery, soldiery
-ful: This suffix creates nouns meaning 'the number of relevant items or the amount of relevant material that can fit in a ~': cupful, cupboardful, handful, houseful, mouthful, spoonful
-iana: Americana, Boswelliana, Churchilliana, cricketana, Nixoniana, Shakespeariana, Victoriana

12.1.5 Agents, Instruments and Patients from Nouns

The suffix -er, which usually has a verb for its base, is also found attached to nouns. The suffix -ist makes agent-like nouns from other nouns as its preferred pattern. The suffix -an frequently makes person nouns from other nouns. These sometimes have an unpredictable extra <i> before the -an. The suffix -ee, which is usually added to verbs, occasionally makes patient nouns on the basis of nouns. Sometimes the bases are shortened before -ee is added. Examples of all of these are given below.

>   -er: cricketer, drummer, footballer
>   -an: grammarian, librarian, musician
>   -ist: artist, harpist, Marxist, pianist, tobacconist, trombonist
>   -ee: biographee

LEVEL

The suffix -er is met early, but less frequently on nominal bases. The suffix -ist will feel familiar to many speakers of other European languages.

12.1.6 Marking Gender

Usually in English, the masculine is unmarked and the specifically feminine is marked; the only potential counter-example is *widower*, derived from *widow*, but here we are not convinced that the -er was originally a gender-marker, though that has become its effect. A few suffixes mark specifically female entities, though none of them can be used freely. Examples are given below.

>   -ess: lioness, tigress, actress, countess, empress, goddess, priestess, princess,
>   shepherdess, stewardess

ADVICE: Although these words are well-established in usage, they tend to be interpreted as denigrating and sexist these days, and are best avoided entirely. *Princess* is, however, in current use in fairy tales and as a form of address to very young girls from family members.

>   -ette: *majorette, shrinkette* ('psychologist'). This is not the most important use
>   of this suffix, and words marking gender using this suffix are definitely
>   derogatory or trivializing.

12.1.7 Marking Inhabitants

The words which are the names for inhabitants are mostly also words which can be used as adjectives, and many of them are also used as the names of languages. A number of examples are listed below with a range of suffixes, but it is hard to predict which suffix will be used on what noun. Some of the extra letters or deletions before the suffixes are unpredictable.

> -an: African, American, Belgian, Burundian, Canadian, Chicagoan, Chilean, Columbian, European, Fijian, Haitian, Hungarian, Italian, Mexican, Roman, Singaporean, Tibetan. When the place ends in <a>, rule S5 applies, and just –n is added, as in Nigerian, Romanian, Russian, Samoan, Syrian, Tunisian, Zambian
> -er: Aucklander, Berliner, Icelander, Londoner, New Yorker
> -ese: Chinese, Congolese, Faroese, Japanese, Maltese, Senegalese, Taiwanese, Vietnamese
> -i: Iraqi, Israeli, Pakistani, Punjabi, Somali, Yemeni
> -ian (probably a variant of -an, but the use of <i> is then unpredictable): Bostonian, Brazilian, Egyptian, Iranian, Norwegian, Panamanian, Parisian, Ukrainian
> -ite: Dunedinite
> with no suffix: Afghan, Dane, Scot, Pole, Swede, Swiss, Thai, Turk

12.1.8 Young, Small, Cute or Worthless

English has a small number of suffixes which are used to indicate that the noun to which they are added is young, small, cute or worthless. These are not very freely used, as they are in many other languages, and it is wiser just to recognize them rather than to try to use them to create new words.

> –ie/-y: This suffix is the only freely used suffix in this set; it is not used to mean 'worthless' and its spelling is variable. Although there are many exceptions, the basic rule is to take the base, keep as much from the beginning of the base as will fit into a single syllable, and then add [i]. This means that *dog* gives *doggie* and *cigarette* gives *ciggy*. Although this affix can be used very freely, it is better for learners to use it only when they have met it, because it tends to sound very child-like or regional (Australian and New Zealand and Scottish varieties of English use these forms more than other varieties). The same affix is used on names (sometimes with the base changed beyond recognition). Some generally accepted examples of both types are given below. Sometimes the spelling is modified to fit the pronunciation, sometimes the pronunciation is changed to fit the spelling.

Examples, ordinary words: aunt > auntie, barbecue > barbie, dad > daddy, football > footie, girl > girlie, goalkeeper > goalie, grandmother > granny, handkerchief > hankie [hæŋki], homeboy > homie, horse > horsie, lad > laddie, lass > lassie, nightgown > nightie (nighty), politician > pollie, present > pressie [prezi], position > possie [pɒzi], rhododendron > rhodie [rɒdi], stomach > tummy

Examples, names (many of these names have other abbreviations as well): Alexander > Sandy, Angela > Angie, Anne > Annie, Catherine > Cathy or Katie or Kitty, Deborah > Debbie, Edward or Theodore > Teddy, Elizabeth > Bessy or Betty or Lizzie, Frederick > Freddy, Helen > Nelly, Jessica > Jessie, John > Johnny, Kenneth > Kenny, Laurence or Lorraine > Laurie, Margaret > Maggie or Peggy, Richard > Dicky, Susan > Susy, Thomas > Tommy, Victoria > Vicky, William > Billy

---

ADVICE: If in doubt about how to spell this suffix, use <ie>, which is the most modern spelling.

-ette: This suffix is always stressed. It can be used to indicate small size: *cigarette, diskette, kitchenette, statuette*; it can also be used of fabrics to indicate that they are not genuine: *flannelette, leatherette, satinette.*

-kin: This suffix is rarely used. Examples include the very unusual words *gherkin, lambkin, ramekin.*

-let: This suffix can be used to indicate a young animal: *piglet*; it can be used to indicate small size: *booklet, droplet, platelet, streamlet, tartlet*; it can also be used to indicate worthlessness: *starlet.*

-ling: This suffix can be used to indicate a young animal: *duckling, gosling* (< goose), *spiderling*; it can also be used to indicate worthlessness: *lordling, princeling.*

-o: Like *-ie* this is added to an abbreviated form, and is more often used in Australian English than elsewhere, though examples are found elsewhere: *ammunition > ammo, combination > combo, journalist > journo, musician > muso, (car) registration > rego* (Australian).

-s: *Debs* (< Deborah), *Jules* (< Julia), *pops* (< pop 'father'). This is sometimes added to *-er* or to *-ie* to give forms such as *champers* (< champagne), *Wimblers* (< Wimbledon) and *walkies*. The suffix is very rare.

12.1.9 Marking Cost

In some words, the suffix *-age* is used to mark the amount of money paid for something. Examples include *cellarage, corkage, porterage, postage, wharfage*. This usage need only be pointed out at advanced levels.

12.1.10 The Suffix -ism

The suffix *-ism* is used to derive nouns mostly denoting a philosophy or way of thinking, a science, a pattern of action, a disease or a way of speaking, either from a name or from another noun. The range of potential meanings here may make understanding these words rather difficult. Nouns in *-ism* very often have a corresponding noun in *-ist* denoting a person who holds the relevant philosophical position, especially when the base is a name. There is also sometimes a corresponding verb in *-ize*. These words tend to be formal, unless they are jocular. Examples include *absenteeism, ageism, alcoholism, Americanism, atheism, authoritarianism, consumerism, Darwinism, hooliganism, jingoism, Marxism, nationalism, Platonism, sexism, socialism.* New words in *-ism* can be created, but sometimes have a trivializing effect, which may not always be desirable: *bossism* does not sound serious.

12.1.11 Some Minor Suffixes

-arian: This suffix sometimes looks like an affix in its own right, and sometimes can be seen as a mixture of *-ary* and *-ian*. It denotes someone who participates in something or holds a particular philosophical position. Rule S2 applies. Examples include *authoritarian, humanitarian, totalitarian, vegetarian, veterinarian.* This suffix is stressed on the <a> [eə].

-eer: This suffix, which is always stressed, denotes a person who deals with something. Examples include *auctioneer, charioteer, engineer, mountaineer, puppeteer.* Some words with this suffix are rather disparaging, but not those cited here.

-nik: This suffix was very fashionable in the early second half of the twentieth century, and now is much less used, though it remains in a few words, often ones denoting fans of something. Examples include *beatnik, folknik* and, with a different meaning, the Russian loan word *sputnik.*

-ster: This suffix is often disparaging in modern words, but need not be in older words. Examples include *fraudster, funster, gangster, jokester, punster.* In US English it is used jokingly on the end of proper names, and always with the definite article *the*, to create nickname-like words.

12.2 Nouns from Verbs

There are many suffixes which derive nouns from verbs. The number of different suffixes, and the choice that is implied by that, makes such words difficult enough to deal with. The meanings of the suffixes are even harder to deal with. There are many meanings that attach to the relevant suffixes, but many meanings attach to each suffix, and many suffixes share the same meanings. This does not imply that all of the suffixes mean precisely the same things; rather, there are overlapping meanings for each suffix. Sometimes a word with a given base and a given suffix can have several meanings. A *diner*, for example, can mean a person who is dining, or who dines, but it can also mean, especially in America, a place where you can eat. A *sleeper* can mean a person who is asleep, but it can also mean a compartment in a train where you are expected to sleep, or the whole carriage which contains such compartments, or the whole train. It can also mean a kind of earring that you put in your ear while you are asleep. A *keeper* can mean a person who keeps things (e.g. who looks after the animals in a zoo), but it can also mean a thing which is worth keeping.

We can divide nouns derived from verbs into two large classes. First there are those where the noun is most likely to mean a person, nearly always a person involved in the action of the verb. So one of the meanings of *diner* is 'a person who is dining'. But very often the same suffixes which create words that denote people, create words which denote animals (a *retriever* is a dog which has been bred to retrieve game when hunting), or machines or things which are involved in the action of the verb (an *amplifier* is a piece of electronic equipment which amplifies sound). They may also denote something or someone involved with the action of the verb, but as the person or thing to whom or to which something happens (see *keeper*, above), and even, as we have seen with *sleeper* and *diner*, the place where the action of the verb takes place.

The second major class of nouns derived from verbs involves what we might call events. A *demonstration* is an event during which something is demonstrated. But such nouns can also denote the product of the action of the verb (a *description* is something which arises when someone describes something), the result of the action of the verb (*inflation* is what happens when prices become inflated), the thing to which something happens (a *payment* is what is made when someone pays someone else), the thing which carries out the action of the verb – where we are now overlapping with the first major set (for example, a *refreshment* is something which refreshes someone), and even the people who carry out the action of the verb (the *administration* is the set of people who administer something). Even this list is not complete.

We will deal with these two major classes of suffix separately. Not every noun created with these suffixes can have every one of these meanings, and some have others as well. Each set of meanings is related, and there is a path of development from one of these meanings to another. But the affixes are fundamentally, most typically, associated with people or with events.

12.3   Suffixes Associated with People

12.3.1   The Suffix -er

The suffix *-er* (in learned words, sometimes *-or*) is the most reliable of these suffixes. You can use it to make up new words meaning 'the person who carries out the action of the verb', especially where the verb is transitive. That person may be carrying out the action of the verb at the time of discussion, be a person who regularly carries out that action or a person who carries out that action on a professional basis. For example, there is a very rare verb, which you are unlikely ever to have met (we have only ever seen it in dictionaries), to *disponge*. You can be fairly sure that if you ever came across this verb, you could invent the word *disponger*, to mean 'a person who disponges (probably regularly or professionally)'.

Rule S4 applies. Rule S2 applies inconsistently. The *-or* version arises particularly after bases that end in <ct>, <pt>, <vise> or in the suffix *-ate*, but it is not always found in these places and can also be found on other verbs, especially in legal contexts.

Examples with *-er*:
compose + -er > composer
deny + -er > denier
disrupt + -er > disrupter
export + -er > exporter
fly + -er > flyer
fry + -er > frier or fryer
interpret + -er > interpreter
kill + -er > killer
lead + -er > leader
manage + -er > manager
paint + -er > painter
provide + -er > provider
sympathize + -er > sympathizer
teach + -er > teacher
torture + -er > torturer

Examples with *-or*:
act + -or > actor
edit + -or > editor
educate + -or > educator
govern + -or > governor
illustrate + -or > illustrator
oppress + -or > oppressor
profess + -or > professor
protect + -or > protector
supervise + -or > supervisor
translate + or > translator

Note that while *lover* in a verbal-nexus compound like *dog-lover* simply means 'a person who loves something', *lover* by itself means 'a person with whom one has a sexual relationship'. A *prayer* is not a person who prays, but the words they utter when they pray. A *waiter* is a person who waits on tables in a café or restaurant.

> POTENTIAL PROBLEM: There are a number of cases where the *-er* suffix creates a form which also has another meaning. The other meaning cannot be worked out on the basis of the *-er* and its base. Some examples are given below.

Examples:

batter	'person who is batting in baseball'	batter	'mixture from which cakes etc. are made'
blazer	'person who blazes something, usu. a trail'	blazer	'man's light jacket'
cutter	'person who or thing which cuts'	cutter	'type of ship'
dresser	'person who helps someone get dressed'	dresser	'piece of furniture'
layer	'person who lays something'	layer	'level, stratum, even thickness'
letter	'person who lets property'	letter	'alphabetical symbol, epistle'
looker	'person who looks'	looker	'person with good looks'
punter	'person who punts a boat'	punter	'customer, gambler'
riser	'person who gets up (early)'	riser	'the vertical part of a step; a vertical pipe'
washer	'person or thing that washes'	washer	'small ring of metal or rubber'

> POTENTIAL PROBLEM: Although *-er* can be used to make nouns denoting people (agents) or things (instruments) and can sometimes show one or the other quite freely, on other occasions only one of the meanings is in general use, and in some cases a meaning which is neither of these is the main meaning of the word.

Examples:

breaker	usually a wave on the shore
cheater	often a garment; a person who cheats is a *cheat*
copier	usually a machine; a person whose job is to copy documents by hand is a *copyist*

dispenser	'machine which provides a measure of some product'
drawer	'part of a piece of furniture for storage'
kneeler	'item on which one kneels'
poker	'card game', 'instrument for stirring the logs or coals in a fire'
sewer [suːə]	'pipe which carries human waste for treatment'
strainer	'a thing which prevents tea-leaves getting into the cup; a thing which holds back solids, while allowing liquids to pass through'
teaser	'a puzzle; something to tempt someone'; a person who teases is a *tease*
toaster	'machine which toasts bread'
tourer	often a car; a person who tours is a *tourist*
wiper	'thing which clears a windscreen so you can see through it during rain'

12.3.2 The Suffix -ee

The suffix *-ee* [iː] is added to verbs to make nouns which denote the direct object or the indirect object of the verb. So an *employee* is a 'person who is employed' and a *payee* is a 'person to whom something is paid'. You may come across other relationships with the verb, but these are the common ones. Words with the suffix *-ee* denote people, except in some rare technical terminologies. This suffix is more common in US English than in British English, and is used rather more flexibly in US English than in British English. It can be used to invent new words especially when it is directly contrasted with a corresponding word in *-er*. So we could invent something like *I'd rather be the puncher than the punchee*. The suffix *-ate* is usually deleted before *-ee*, unless that would put a <c> or a <g> immediately before the *-ee* (we find *dedicatee* rather than *★dedicee*). Spelling rule S4 applies. This suffix is always stressed.

Examples:
address + -ee > addressee 'person to whom something is addressed'
consign + -ee > consignee 'person to whom something is consigned'
detain + -ee > detainee 'person detained (by the police)'
draft + -ee > draftee 'person who is drafted (into the armed forces)'
employ + -ee > employee 'person employed'
evacuate + -ee > evacuee 'person who is evacuated (e.g. from a war zone)'
franchise + -ee > franchisee 'person to whom something is franchised'
nominate + -ee > nominee 'person who is nominated'
pay + -ee > payee 'person to whom money is paid'
promise + ee > promisee 'person to whom something is promised'
train + -ee > trainee 'person being trained'

POTENTIAL PROBLEM: There are quite a few established words which end in <ee> which do not represent this affix. This would not be problematic if they did not look as though they had a base and an affix. So *coffee* is not a problem, because there is no verb *coff*. In some other cases matters are less clear, and in some instances, the <ee> is pronounced [eɪ].

Examples:

committee [kəˈmɪtiː] 'group of people called to discuss a problem'

fiancé(e) [fiːˈɒnseɪ] 'man (woman) to whom one is engaged to be married'

guarantee [gærənˈtiː] 'a promise, esp. of the standard of goods'

protegee [ˈprɒtɪʒeɪ] (or written in French as *protégée*) 'person to whom an experienced person gives guidance'

puttee [ˈpʌtiː] 'a legging'

settee [sɪˈtiː] 'a sofa, couch'

12.3.3   The Suffix -ant

The suffix *-ant*, sometimes, not always predictably, spelt <ent>, is mostly added to quite formal bases to produce nouns. The nouns can denote people or instruments, as one might expect. Many words with this suffix have unrecognizable bases. The suffix *-ate* is sometimes removed before *-ant* is added. Rule S4 applies. Rule S2 applies. You cannot invent new words on this pattern, but may need to recognize them. Many of these words have quite specific meanings, which are not entirely predictable from the elements in the word.

Examples:

aspire + -ant > aspirant	'person who desires to join some group'
attend + -ant> attendant	'person who looks after something or someone'
celebrate + -ant > celebrant	'person whose job is to manage a formal celebration'
consult + ant > consultant	'person whose job is to provide advice (be consulted)'
cool + -ant > coolant	'something used to cool an engine or machine'
defend + -ant > defendant	'person defending themselves in a court of law'
descend + -ant > descendant	'person who is one's child or a child of one's child, etc.'
determine + -ant > determinant	'thing which determines whether someone or something is suitable for something'

inhabit + -ant > inhabitant	'person who lives in a place'
preside + -ant > president	'leader of a country or of an organization'
reside + -ant > resident	'person who lives in a building, town, etc.'
serve +-ant > servant	'person who is employed to look after someone'
vary + -ant > variant	'thing which varies in a scientific statement; a slightly different version'

POTENTIAL PROBLEM: Because the suffix *-ant* (or *-ent*) is also used to create adjectives, it is not always clear whether a word with this suffix is an adjective or a noun or both. The word *assailant* is a noun, *defiant* is an adjective and *repellant* can be either. *Student* is a noun (note that the <y> from *study* has been deleted in this word and that the first vowel has an unpredictable quality), *coherent* is an adjective and *resident* can be either.

12.4 Suffixes Primarily Denoting Events

It must be remembered that although the set of suffixes dealt with here primarily denote events, they may denote all kinds of other things as well. In individual instances, the event reading may be extremely rare or non-existent. Very few of these affixes are reliable, in the sense that they can be freely used and that the learner can be sure that a particular form will be part of the language. Most have to be learned as individual words, though recognizing the suffixes may aid understanding. The examples below are organized according to this distinction.

12.4.1 Suffixes Which Can Be Used Freely

-ing: All verbs which are not modal verbs (see Chapter 7) have a corresponding nominal form in *-ing*, and the form is totally predictable (see Chapter 8).

POTENTIAL PROBLEM: Although nouns in *-ing* are very common and can often cover a number of the readings of event nouns, some nouns in *-ing* have strongly preferred readings. Some examples are given below.

Examples:
coupling	instrument
covering	instrument
dripping	result 'cold fat from roast meat'

dwelling	location
heating	instrument
lighting	instrument
living	result 'amount of money allowing one to live; a job providing this'
lodging	location
meaning	abstract cause
packaging	instrument
tubing	collective
wedding	ceremony
wrestling	sport associated with (also boxing, swimming, skiing, etc.)
writing	result

In many cases, the preferred readings of -*ing* forms are adjectives (see Section 14.2.2). In most of these cases, other readings are possible in context, but one is much more usual than the rest.

-ation: There is an argument as to whether this is best treated as a suffix -*ion* which sometimes has an -*at*- preceding it, or as a single suffix. In either case, -*ion*, -*ition*, -*sion* and -*cation* seem to be alternative forms of the same affix, and the only forms which are reliably available are those ending in -*ation*. All verbs ending in -*ize* can take -*ation* (*civilize* > *civilization*), and all verbs that end in -*ify* can take -*cation* (*justify* > *justification*). Note that the nominalization for *aggrandise* is *aggrandisement*, which is an apparent exception, though one that was borrowed. Although -*ation* appears in a lot of other nouns, its occurrence there has to be treated as something irregular, not something which can be predicted. The suffix -*ation* is always stressed on the <a>. Note that there is sometimes a change to the vowel in the base or an extra <i> before the suffix. Rules S4 and S2 apply.

Examples with -*ation*:
acculturate + -ation > acculturation
classify + -ation > classification
consider + -ation > consideration
defame + -ation > defamation
fortify + -ation > fortification
gratify + -ation > gratification
idolize + -ation > idolization
inhale + -ation > inhalation
nasalize + -ation > nasalization
perturb + -ation > perturbation
present + -ation > presentation [prezən'teɪʃən]

pronounce + -ation > pronunciation
rarify + -ation > rarification
reveal + -ation > revelation [revəˈleɪʃən]
specialize + -ation > specialization
utilize + -ation > utilization

Examples with other forms of the affix:
act + -ation > action
add + -ation > addition
commit + -ation > commission
compete + -ation > competition
complete + -ation > completion
discuss + -ation > discussion
evade + -ation > evasion
expand + -ation > expansion
expel + -ation > expulsion
instruct + -ation > instruction
invent + -ation > invention
oppose + -ation > opposition
oppress + -ation > oppression
predict + -ation > prediction
revert + -ation > reversion
scan + -ation > scansion

12.4.2 Suffixes Which Can Be Recognized, But Not Used Freely

-age: Most of the words with this suffix are rather rare, and the commonest ones have meanings which are unpredictable. Rules S4 and S2 apply.

Examples:
carry + -age > carriage 'vehicle; cost of transport; act of transporting'
cover + -age > coverage 'amount covered'
leak + -age > leakage 'material which leaks'
marry + -age > marriage 'state of being married'
moor + -age > moorage 'place for mooring'
spoil + -age > spoilage 'things spoiled and so wasted'
wreck + -age > wreckage 'material left when something is wrecked'
-al: The suffix -al makes nouns from verbs which are stressed on their final syllable (but not from all such verbs). The only exception is burial < [ˈberi], which, historically speaking, does not contain the same suffix. Rules S4, S3 and S2 apply.

Examples:
acquit + -al > acquittal
appraise + -al > appraisal
approve + -al > approval
arrive + -al > arrival
deny + -al > denial
propose + -al > proposal
refuse + -al > refusal
rehearse + -al > rehearsal
remove + -al > removal
survive + -al > survival
try + -al > trial
withdraw + -al > withdrawal

> POTENTIAL PROBLEM: There are many nouns derived from adjectives ending in -*al*, and these are distinct from the nouns listed above. Examples include *intellectual, labial, local, official, physical.*

-ance/-ancy/-ence/-ency: The precise form of this suffix is not predictable in English, and sometimes two forms may co-exist with the same or contrasting meanings. Where these forms exist, there is often an adjective in -*ant*/-*ent*, as well. Rules S4 and S3 apply.

Examples:

Example	*Adjective*	*Comment*
ascend + -ance > ascendance	ascendant	
ascend + -ancy > ascendancy		This is probably the most usual of the forms from *ascend*
ascend + -ence > ascendence	ascendent	
ascend + -ency > ascendency		
assist + -ance > assistance		
clear + -ance > clearance		
depend + -ence > dependence	dependent	
depend + -ency > dependency		Can also mean a country which is ruled by another
diverge + -ence > divergence	divergent	
occur + -ence > occurrence [əˈkʌrəns]	occurrent	

Example	*Adjective*	*Comment*
perform + –ance > performance		
reside + –ence > residence ['rezɪdəns]	resident	When a location, any place where someone lives
reside + –ency > residency ['rezɪdənsi]		When a location, usually an official home of e.g. an ambassador

–ment: There are hundreds of nouns which end in –*ment*, mostly derived from verbs with stress on the last syllable.

Examples:

agree + –ment > agreement	
align + –ment > alignment	
commence + –ment > commencement	In America, specifically 'a ceremony where students receive their diplomas, etc.'
commit + –ment > commitment	
confine + –ment > confinement	In old texts 'the period during which a woman is giving birth'
develop + –ment > development	
displace + –ment > displacement	
govern + –ment > government	'the body which governs a country'
mange + –ment > management	Can mean 'the people who manage' as well as 'the process of managing'
move + –ment > movement	
pay + –ment > payment	Often, 'the money used to pay for something'
state + –ment > statement	
treat + –ment > treatment	Especially being treated by a doctor for a medical problem

–ure: In many instances, the 'event' reading of these words is rather rare. Note that sometimes there is an extra <t> before the suffix, and that the phonology is not always predictable.

Examples:

create + –ure > creature [kri:ʧə]	'animal'
depart + –ure > departure	
fail + –ure > failure	
fix + –ure > fixture	also, 'an arranged sporting event'

mix + -ure > mixture	'something which contains many things mixed together'
please + -ure > pleasure [pleʒə]	'the emotion that is the result of being pleased'
press + -ure > pressure ['preʃə]	'the force exerted by something against something which it is touching'
sculpt + -ure > sculpture	'a statue', the result of the sculpting process

12.5 Nouns from Adjectives

Most nouns which are formed on an adjectival base mean 'the state or quality of being ~' where the swung dash shows the meaning of the adjective involved. For example, *niceness* can be glossed as the 'the quality of being nice' and *humanity* can be glossed as 'the state of being human'. Most of the suffixes which can be added to adjectives to make nouns can also be added to other types of base, but some prefer this kind of base. Some nouns corresponding to adjectives have idiosyncratic forms which cannot be predicted. Some examples are given below.

Examples:

dead	death
heavy	weight (*heaviness* is also possible)
high	height
sorry	sorrow
young	youth

12.5.1 The Major Patterns: -ness and -ity

The suffixes -*ness* and -*ity* are the major suffixes deriving nouns from adjectives. Of the two, -*ity* is the more restricted. It forms learned nouns, and is usually added to learned adjectives, e.g. adjectives ending in, for instance, -*able*, -*al*, -*ible*, -*ic*, -*ive*, -*ous* (which often takes the form -*os*- before -*ity*). The suffix -*ness* has a far wider usage, even being possible on words which usually take -*ity*, though not always with the same meaning. Sometimes nouns in -*ity* have an unexpected meaning, or are more technical, while the meaning of words in -*ness* tends to be more predictable. The stress on words ending in -*ity* is often different from the stress on the base, while the stress on -*ness* words is always the same as the stress on the base. Spelling rule S4 applies before -*ity*. Spelling rule S2 applies before -*ness*. Pronunciation rule P1 applies before -*ity*, and there are some irregularities in form with -*ity*.

Examples:

aware + -ness > awareness

blue + -ness > blueness

brief + -ity > brevity

complex + -ity > complexity

curious + -ity > curiosity — 'a desire to know things'

extreme + -ity > extremity — 'the furthest extent of something, [eksˈtremɪti]   an end'

foolish + -ness > foolishness

happy + -ness > happiness

hopeless + -ness > hopelessness

incomplete + ness > incompleteness

monstrous + -ity > monstrosity — 'something large and ugly'

new + -ness > newness

obscene + -ity > obscenity [əbˈsenɪti] — 'the quality of being obscene; a rude word or utterance'

odd + -ity > oddity — 'an odd thing'

odd + -ness > oddness — 'the quality of being odd'

peculiar + -ity > peculiarity — 'the quality of being peculiar; [pɪkjuːliˈærɪti]   something that distinguishes one item from other similar ones'

peculiar + -ness > peculiarness — 'the quality of being peculiar'

polite + -ness > politeness

probable + -ity > probability — 'the quality or degree of being probable; used often in statistics'

probable + -ness > probableness — 'the quality of being probable'

productive + -ity > productivity — 'the quality of being productive, esp. in economics or linguistics'

productive + -ness > productiveness — 'the quality of being productive'

real + -ity > reality

round + -ness > roundness

senile + -ity > senility

silly + -ness > silliness

stupid + -ity > stupidity [stjuːˈpɪdɪti]

stupid + -ness > stupidness

voracious [vəˈreɪʃəs] + -ity > voracity [vəˈræsɪti]

willing + -ness > willingness

ADVICE: If in doubt, use *-ness* rather than *-ity*, but when you have come across a word with *-ity* in a particular usage (especially a technical one), do not replace it with the corresponding *-ness* word. Where the normal word ends in *-ity*, the word in *-ness* sounds odd, but remains comprehensible.

Although -*ness* has a very regular meaning, there are a very few cases where the meaning of a word in -*ness* is not predictable.

Examples:

busy + -ness > business [ˈbɪznɪs]	'commerce, trade'; the noun from *busy* is sometimes written as *busy-ness*
good + -ness > goodness	Also a mild expression of surprise
high + -ness > highness	'a title for a royal person'; the ordinary noun from *high* is *height*
ill + -ness > illness	Also 'disease'
like + -ness > likeness	'similarity'; also, in old texts, 'portrait'
open + -ness > openness	More likely to be used of a person's character ('honesty, willingness to accept new experiences') or of countryside than of, say, a door
sick + -ness > sickness	Also 'disease'

The suffix -*ness* is also used on other word-classes, but such words are rare and often slightly odd: *fewness, muchness, oneness, otherness, thereness, twoness.*

12.5.2   The Suffix -th

The suffix -*th* can be found on a limited number of adjective bases, very often with an unpredictable change of vowel in the base (see Section 17.2.1). Most of these nouns are in common usage, and although the -*th* can sometimes be replaced by -*ness* (with no vowel change), it is better to learn these as irregular forms.

Examples:
deep + -th > depth
long + -th > length
broad + -th > breadth
strong + -th > strength
wide + -th > width
warm + -th > warmth
true + -th > truth

12.5.3   The Suffix -ism

Although it is not always easy to recognize, because often words in -*ism* denote a philosophy or set of beliefs (e.g. *Mohammedanism, separatism*), or a linguistic expression (e.g. *Americanism, colloquialism*), there are occasions on which -*ism* forms a state or quality noun from adjectives, sometimes in variation with -*ity*. Some examples are given below. Note that sometimes an adjectival suffix appears to have been deleted. The pronunciation rule P1 applies before -*ism*.

Examples:
athletic + –ism > athleticism
heroic + –ism > heroism
magnetic + –ism > magnetism
namby-pamby + –ism > namby-pambyism
rowdy + –ism > rowdyism
synchronic + –ism > synchronism (synchronicity has a specialized, related meaning)
tribal + –ism > tribalism
true + –ism > truism 'a statement which is obviously true'

12.5.4 Other Suffixes

Other suffixes which are more commonly used with other word-classes in the base are also occasionally used with adjective bases. Although the word parts may be familiar here, the patterns of use should not be copied, but these words should be seen as irregular.

> -age: shortage ('a situation where resources are insufficient')
> -cy: celibacy (from *celibate*), literacy (from *literate*), normalcy (US; *normality* means the same thing), obstinacy (from *obstinate*)
> -dom: freedom, wisdom (from *wise*)
> -ery: bravery (in cases like *finery* and *greenery*, the noun denotes a collection of things)
> -hood: falsehood ('a lie'), likelihood ('probability')
> -ice: justice
> -ship: hardship ('poverty, the lack of necessities')
> -y: difficulty, honesty, jealousy

For relationships between nouns and adjectives with no suffix, see Section 17.1.2
Sometimes affixes are added to adjectives with meanings other than those discussed above, typically the meaning the affix has when attached to a different class of bases. Some examples have already been given with *-ism* in Section 12.5.3. Some other examples are given below.

> -er: commoner
> -ery: greenery
> -ese: Americanese, legalese
> -ie: this diminutive marker is sometimes added to adjectives to make a noun meaning 'a person or thing which is ~', often with overtones of affection or disparagement. Examples include: *dearie* (often a term of address), *goody* ('person who is on the side of right and justice'), *littlie* ('small child',

regional), *meanie* ('unpleasant person'), *pinkie* ('the smallest finger', esp. US or Scottish English), *smoothie* ('drink made with fruit and dairy produce'), *weirdie* (more usually *weirdo*, 'strange person')

-ist: educationalist, extremist, positivist, purist, specialist

-ling: weakling, youngling (rare)

-ment: oddment 'something left over'

-ster: youngster

13

MAKING VERBS

13.1 Making Verbs with Suffixes

13.1.1 The Suffixes -ize and -ify

These two suffixes are the most important verb-creating suffixes. For the most part, where one is used the other cannot occur, and vice versa; there are very few cases where both are possible, and if they are, they are usually synonymous. Their meanings are also parallel, though quite complex. Often on adjectives they mean 'to make ~' (*equalize* means 'to make equal'), and on nouns they have a range of meanings including 'to provide with ~' (as in *computerize*), 'to make into ~' (as in *colonize*), 'to become ~' (as in *acidify*), 'to put into ~' (as in *containerize*). The crucial point about verbs with these suffixes is the stress pattern of the word created. The new words, if they are three syllables long, will have a pattern of stressed-unstressed-secondary stressed, and if they are four syllables long will have one of the patterns unstressed-stressed-unstressed-secondary stressed (*humidify*) or stressed-unstressed-unstressed-secondary stressed (*alphabetize*). There is sometimes some modification to the base (deletion or addition) to guarantee such patterns. In particular, a final [i] is often lost before these suffixes (rule S2). There are occasional exceptions to these patterns (and, of course, some longer words, which tend to finish with these patterns). There are many words with both affixes whose bases are not English words.

Examples:
anthology + –ize > anthologize ('make into or put into an anthology')
apology + –ize > apologize ('make an apology (for)')
beauty + –ify > beautify ('make beautiful')
class + –ify > classify ['klæsɪfaɪ] ('put into classes')

diary + -ize > diarize ('put into one's diary')
diverse + -ify > diversify ('make (more) diverse')
dramatic + -ize > dramatize ('make dramatic')
general + -ize > generalize
hypothesis + -ize > hypothesize
immobile + -ize > immobilize ('make immobile')
italics + -ize > italicize ('put into italics')
motor + -ize > motorize ('provide with a motor')
mummy + -ify > mummify ('make into an (Egyptian) mummy')
object + -ify > objectify ('treat as an object')
oxygen + -ize > oxygenize ('add oxygen to')
pure + -ify > purify ('make pure')
revolution + -ize > revolutionize ('change in a revolutionary way')
simple + -ify > simplify
social + ize > socialize ('teach how to be sociable; mix socially (with)')
solid + -ify > solidify ('make solid, become solid')
special + -ize > specialize
stable + -ize > stabilize ('make stable')

13.1.2 The suffix -ate

The suffix -ate [eɪt] is added to nouns and adjectives to make verbs. Many verbs whose base is not an English word have identical written forms acting as nouns or adjectives, but then without the full vowel [eɪ] in the suffix. For example, the verb graduate ['grædjʊeɪt] has the corresponding noun graduate ['grædjʊɪt]. When added to adjectives, the suffix usually means 'to make ~', so that domesticate means 'to make domestic, i.e. tame'. When added to nouns, -ate has a range of meanings, comparable to those of -ize and -ify.

Examples:
active + -ate > activate ('make active')
alien + -ate > alienate ('take away from someone something which by right is theirs; to take away support or friendship')
assassin + -ate > assassinate ('to murder a high-profile person')
carbon + -ate > carbonate ('add carbon dioxide to')
different + -ate > differentiate ('distinguish from similar things')
granule + -ate > granulate ('make into granules')
luxury + -ate > luxuriate ('live in luxury')
urine + -ate > urinate ('to pass urine')
vaccine + -ate > vaccinate ('administer a vaccine to')

There are a few instances where -ate appears to have been added to a verb, but such words are probably created from the -ation noun.

Examples:
administration − –ion > administrate
commutation − –ion > commutate ('commute; reduce the severity of a punishment')

13.1.3   The Suffix -en

The suffix *-en* can be found added to adjectives, but nearly always ones containing just one syllable and ending in a plosive or a fricative. It means 'make ~'. Note that *heighten* and *lengthen* have nouns in the base rather than adjectives, but the corresponding adjectives do not end in a plosive or a fricative. Rules S3 and S4 apply.

Examples:
awake + -en > awaken
broad + -en > broaden
dark + -en > darken
fat + -en > fatten
fright + -en > frighten ('scare')
heart + -en > hearten ('give courage to')
height + -en > heighten (of something abstract) ('make higher or stronger')
length + -en > lengthen ('make longer')
mad + -en > madden
ripe + -en > ripen
tight + -en > tighten
weak + -en > weaken
wide + -en > widen

There are a few cases where the verb is formed not just with the suffix *-en* but with a simultaneous prefix *en-* and suffix *-en*. In the case of *enlighten*, the verb means 'cast metaphorical light on something; to explain to someone', whereas *lighten* means 'to make lighter (in weight)'.

Examples:
bold + en- ... -en > embolden
light + en- ... -en > enlighten
live + en- ... -en > enliven ('make more lively')

LEVEL
All of these suffixes will be met fairly early, but need not be used until much later in the acquisition process. Words with the suffixes *-ate* and *-en* have to be learnt as individual items.

13.2   Making Verbs with Prefixes

There are a number of prefixes which can be added to nouns to make verbs. These are mostly negative prefixes, and mean 'remove ~ from' or 'remove from ~', but there are also others. These are unusual in the system of English, since usually the word-class to which the word belongs is determined by a suffix rather than by a prefix. Examples with negative prefixes are given below.

Examples:
de- + bug > debug 'to remove the "bugs" from a computer program'
de- + fame > defame 'to spoil someone's fame or reputation'
dis- + arm > disarm 'to remove weapons from'
dis- + courage > discourage 'to remove someone's courage, to daunt'
dis- + mast > dismast 'to knock over the mast of a ship'
dis- + place > displace 'to put in another (often unsuitable) place, remove from its usual site, lose'
un- + seat > unseat 'to remove from a seat; (of a horse) to throw the rider'
un- + earth > unearth 'to dig out of the earth' (often figurative)
un- + frock > unfrock 'to remove a priest from the priesthood', also defrock
un- + hand > unhand 'to remove one's hand from (usu. a person)'; now old or humorous
un- + horse > unhorse 'to knock someone off a horse'
un- + latch > unlatch 'to open the latch of'
un- + yoke > unyoke 'to remove the yoke from oxen etc.'

The prefix *en-* (with *em-* before bilabials in most cases) can be added to nouns to make a verb meaning 'to put into ~' and to adjectives to make a verb meaning 'to make ~'. Examples are below.

Examples:
en- + able > enable 'to make capable'
en- + bark >embark 'to go aboard a ship; to put aboard a ship'
en- + circle > encircle 'to form a circle (e.g. of soldiers) around'
en- + code > encode 'to put into code'
en- + large > enlarge 'to make bigger'
en- + plane > emplane 'to go aboard a plane; to put on board a plane'
en- + power > empower 'to make powerful'
en- + rich > enrich 'to make rich'
en- + tomb > entomb 'to put into a tomb'

Sometimes this prefix can be spelt <in>, but note that *ensure* 'make sure' and *insure* 'protect against financial loss' have different meanings.

The prefix *be-* is found on bases that are nouns and adjectives, as well as on verbs, and the meaning is often obscure. No new verbs can be formed with this prefix, and individual words including it have to be learnt as simple items.

Examples:
be- + calm > becalm (usu. passive, of a ship), 'be left in calm waters with no wind'
be- + foul > befoul 'to make foul'
be- + friend > befriend 'to make a friend of'
be- + jewel > bejewel 'to cover in jewels'
be- + little > belittle 'to make someone feel inadequate'
be- + wig > bewig (usu. passive) 'to wear a wig'
be- + witch > bewitch 'to have a magical effect on'

14

MAKING ADJECTIVES

Adjectives can be made from nouns (*parent* + *al* > *parental*), from verbs (*bore* + *ing* > *boring*) and from other adjectives (*green* + *ish* > *greenish*). We do not have to worry about any other patterns. Within each of these patterns, there are some which are easily extendable to new forms, and many more where you should recognize the patterns, but cannot use them yourself to invent new words.

14.1 Adjectives from Nouns

14.1.1 The Suffix -y

The suffix -*y* can be added to mean 'of the nature of ~, having the quality of ~' (where the swung dash indicates the meaning of the noun in the base). It is usually used with basic nouns and never with a noun ending in <y>. Where the base ends in <er>, the <e> may be deleted in well-established words (rule P3) A final silent <e> is deleted before the <y>. Rule S6 may apply.

> Examples:
> anger + -y > angry
> cream + -y > creamy
> grease + -y > greasy
> health + -y > healthy
> hunger + -y > hungry
> luck + -y >lucky
> meat + -y > meaty
> pillow + -y > pillowy
> swamp + -y > swampy
> thirst + -y > thirsty

Overuse of such adjectives may sound child-like, because this is a favourite strategy for making adjectives with young children (in this it is like the use of the homophonous diminutive suffix *-ie*; see Section 12.1.8). Nevertheless, it is a fairly safe way of making new words, and can be used fairly early on in the learning process. Note that some well-established words made in this way have unpredictable meanings.

Examples:

booze + -y > boozy	'where large amounts of alcohol are consumed'
bust + -y > busty	'having a large bosom'
cat + -y > catty	'(of words) hurtful, cruel'
crumb + -y > crumby/ crummy	'of poor quality'
dot + -y > dotty	'silly, mad'
ease + -y > easy	'simple, not requiring hard work'
fish + -y > fishy	'suspicious'
head + -y > heady	'(of a smell, a drink) intoxicating'
heart + -y > hearty	'(of a meal) large; (of appetite) healthy; (of congratulations) heart-felt'
horn + -y > horny	'sexually excited'
mouse + -y > mousy (or mousey)	'of the colour of a mouse'
peak + -y > peaky	'in mild poor health'
rat + -y > ratty	'untidy, worn, angry'

POTENTIAL PROBLEM: There are many words ending in *-y* which are not adjectives, or, if they are adjectives, are not derived in this way. Words like *pretty*, *ready*, *silly* are adjectives, but have no *-y* suffix, because there is no base *prett-*, *read-* or *sill-* with an appropriate meaning.

14.1.2 The Suffix *-ish*

The suffix *-ish* can be reliably added to nouns to make an adjective meaning 'resembling a ~'. It is not added to nouns that end in <sh>, [ʃ]. Spelling rules S2, S3 and S4 apply.

Examples:
amateur + -ish > amateurish
baby + -ish > babyish
boy + -ish > boyish

colt + -ish > coltish
fiend + -ish > fiendish
girl + -ish > girlish
man + -ish > mannish
prude + -ish > prudish
rogue + -ish > roguish

Note that some well-established words made in this way have unpredictable meanings.

Examples:
bear + -ish > bearish   'having poor manners; expecting a fall in prices'
book + -ish > bookish   'reading a lot'
child + -ish > childish   'like a child, but in a bad way'
liver + -ish > liverish   'irritable'
sheep + -ish> sheepish   'embarrassed'
wasp + -ish> waspish   'bad-tempered'

POTENTIAL PROBLEM: There is another -*ish* which marks languages and nationalities, which is also based on nouns, but whose use cannot be extended. In some cases, the <ish> has been shortened to just <sh>, and in some old cases there is a vowel change, too. These just have to be learnt as irregular forms. For practical purposes, *Dutch* and *French* can be viewed as containing variants of this affix.

Examples:
Angle (the original Germanic inhabitants of eastern England) + -ish > English
Cornwall + -ish > Cornish
Dane + -ish > Danish
Ireland +-ish > Irish
Lett + -ish > Lettish (now usually Latvian)
Pole + -ish > Polish
Scot + -ish > Scottish
Spain + -ish > Spanish ['spænɪʃ]
Swede + -ish > Swedish
Wales + -ish > Welsh

14.1.3   The Suffix -esque

The suffix -*esque* [esk] can be freely added to the names of famous people to make fairly formal adjectives meaning 'in the style of ~'. This suffix is always stressed.

Examples:
Caravaggio + -esque > Caravaggioesque
Dante + -esque > Dantesque
Dickens + -esque > Dickensesque
Disney + -esque > Disneyesque
Kipling + -esque > Kiplingesque
Titian + -esque > Titianesque

Note that *Junoesque*, used of a woman, means 'large, buxom and good-looking'.

POTENTIAL PROBLEM: The suffix *-esque* is also added to nouns that are not names, and this usage is not as freely available. Some words carrying this affix have a mocking tone, or are intended to be humorous and non-serious.

Examples:
bimbo + -esque > bimboesque
kindergarten + -esque > kindergartenesque
picture + -esque > picturesque
sculpture + -esque > sculptureseque
statue + -esque > statuesque
teacher + -esque > teacheresque

14.1.4   *The Element* -like

The element *-like* (which may be seen as part of a compound or as a suffix) can be added freely to nouns to make an adjective meaning 'resembling ~'. Where this contrasts with *-y* and *-ish*, the form in *-like* will probably be the most neutral choice, while the others will carry emotional force of some kind. For instance, *childish* is a bad thing to be, but *child-like* is a good thing to be; this is an extreme example, but *-like* is usually extremely transparent in its meaning.

Examples:
business + -like > businesslike
cat + -like > catlike
dream + -like > dreamlike
god + -like > godlike
lady + -like > ladylike
son + -like > sonlike
spring + -like > springlike
sylph + -like > sylphlike
workman + -like > workmanlike

14.1.5 The Suffix -ful

The suffix *-ful* added to nouns makes adjectives meaning 'containing, displaying or in accordance with ~'. It is most often used with nouns denoting emotions, but has wider uses as well. You should recognize this suffix, but should avoid inventing new words using this suffix.

> Examples:
> beauty + -ful > beautiful
> colour + -ful > colourful
> event + -ful > eventful
> faith + -ful > faithful
> hope + -ful > hopeful
> law + -ful > lawful
> mercy + -ful > merciful
> power + -ful > powerful
> purpose + -ful > purposeful
> sloth + -ful > slothful
> success + -ful > successful
> use + -ful > useful
> youth + -ful > youthful

Note that *awful* (historically from *awe* + *ful*) now means 'terrible'.

14.1.6 The Suffix -less

The suffix *-less* [lɪs] makes adjectives meaning 'lacking, not having, free of ~'. The words with *-less* are often antonyms of words with *-ful*. For comparison with *-free*, see Section 14.1.7 below. You need to be able to recognize this suffix, and you can use it yourself. Established words with this suffix often have quite restricted collocations (e.g. *baseless allegation / assertion / charge / complaint / fear / speculation, thankless job / role / task*).

> Examples:
> base + -less > baseless
> end + -less > endless
> god + -less > godless
> hope + -less > hopeless
> law + -less > lawless
> mercy + -less > merciless
> ruth + -less > ruthless
> sense + -less > senseless
> state + -less > stateless

thank + -less > thankless
use + -less > useless
value + -less > valueless

14.1.7 The Element -free

The element *-free* (which can be viewed as an affix or a compound element) makes denominal adjectives meaning 'free from, not containing ~'. It contrasts with *-less* in that adjectives in *-free* imply that it is a good thing not to contain what is in the base, while adjectives in *-less* are far more neutral in this regard. Adjectives in *-free* are widely used in advertising, product descriptions, medical and ecological discussions. A slogan such as *95% fat-free* meaning 'containing 5% fat' is self-contradictory propaganda. You can invent new forms using this formula.

Examples:
care + -free > carefree
duty + -free > duty-free ('not subject to taxes at an international border')
fat + free > fat-free
gluten + -free > gluten-free
lactose + -free > lactose-free
lead + -free > lead-free
scot (an old word meaning 'tax') + -free > scot-free ('without penalty')
sugar + -free > sugar-free

The word *fancy-free* means 'not constrained in one's choices' and is stressed on the *free*.

14.1.8 The Suffix -al or -ar

These suffixes are usually added to learned words, and the variant with <r> is usually found if the base contains an <l>, but there are occasional exceptions (compare *familial* and *familiar*). Although it is useful to recognize these suffixes as creating adjectives, you should use only words which you have already seen on this pattern, and not make up your own. Many words with these suffixes may show a different stress pattern from that of the base. If the suffix *-al* is added to a base that ends in *-a*, one of the <a>s is dropped (rule S5). A final <ce> in the noun in the base is often replaced with a <t> in the adjective, as in *essence* > *essential*. Many other instances of deletion at the boundary are found, as are changes of pronunciation. Many of these words are originally borrowed from Latin, and their form and pronunciation are based on the Latin.

Examples:

baptism + -al > baptismal

diphthong + -al > diphthongal [dɪf θɒŋɡəl]

faeces (US <feces>) + -al > fecal

globe + -al > global

line + -ar > linear ['lɪnɪə]

malaria + -al > malarial

medulla + -ar > medullar

norm + -al > normal

parent + -al > parental

person + -al > personal

plane + -ar > planar [pleɪnə]

tradition + -al > traditional

trivia + -al > trivial

uvula + -ar > uvular

vestige + -al > vestigial [vesˈtɪdʒəl]

zodiac + -al > zodiacal

POENTIAL PROBLEM: It is often the case that an <i> or a <u> is inserted before the suffix -*al*, and this is fundamentally unpredictable.

Examples:

president + -al > presidential

sex + -al > sexual

sequence + -al > sequential

professor + -al > professorial

substance + -al > substantial

office + -al > official [əˈfɪʃəl]

race + -al > racial [reɪʃəl]

angle + ar > angular

POTENTIAL PROBLEM: It is often the case that there are adjectives ending in -*ic* and adjectives ending in -*ical*, and it is in principle impossible to decide which is the right one to use. In some instances, only one is used (e.g. *theatrical*, but *atomic*). In many instances both are possible (e.g. *comic* and *comical*), but even when both are possible, it is often the case that one of them is preferred (even very strongly preferred) in particular subject areas. In linguistics, for example, we find *phonetic*, *phonological*, *pragmatic*, *syntactic* and *semantic* (though alternative forms may be found in old texts or from people who are not linguists). Only a few of these adjectives are genuinely semantically different.

---

historic 'very important in history'   historical 'recorded in history'
economic 'to do with economics'   economical 'saving money'
classic 'of established excellence'   classical 'of ancient Greece or Rome'

14.1.9   The Suffix -ic

The suffix -*ic* [ɪk] is used mainly to create formal, scientific or learned adjectives, frequently on the basis of foreign nouns. In some cases, you may not be able to recognize the base to which the -*ic* is added. Although the suffix is occasionally used to create new words (sometimes even not on foreign bases), you should treat this suffix as one to be recognized and not one that can be used freely to invent new words. On the distinction between -*ic* and -*ical*, see above. Except in a few cases, the stress falls on the syllable before the -*ic* suffix. The exceptions are *Arabic* ['ærəbɪk], *catholic* ['kæθ(ə)lɪk], *chivalric* ['ʃɪvəlrɪk]. When the -*ic* forms a noun rather than an adjective this stress rule may appear to be broken: *heretic* ['herətɪk], *rhetoric* ['retərɪk]. There is often some change, addition or deletion of letters before the suffix. Rule S4 applies, but sometimes a CL/Cs is inserted to split up sequences of vowels instead. A base-final <y> is deleted before -*ic*.

Examples:
alcohol + -ic > alcoholic
algebra + -ic > algebraic [ældʒɪ'breɪk]
anorexia + -ic > anorexic
aroma + -ic > aromatic
democrat + -ic > democratic
economy + -ic > economic
gene + -ic > genetic
history + -ic > historic
lethargy + -ic > lethargic [lɪ'θɑːdʒɪk]
metre + -ic > metric
onomatopoeia + -ic > onomatopoetic or onomatopoeic
pedant + -ic > pedantic
photograph + -ic > photographic
problem + -ic > problematic
realist + -ic > realistic
strategy + -ic > strategic
sulphur + -ic > sulphuric
syntax + -ic > syntactic
volcano + -ic > volcanic [vɒl'kænɪk]

14.1.10   The Suffix -an

The suffix -*an* attaches especially to proper nouns, creating general adjectives from those nouns, and hence the names of inhabitants and languages from proper nouns denoting countries or regions. It is also used on common nouns. In unpredictable cases, an extra <i> is added before the -*an* suffix. Words ending in <a> lose that <a> when the -*an* suffix is added (rule S5). There are sometimes changes at the boundary between the base and the suffix, and sometimes changes in stress. New words may be invented with this suffix when the base ends in <a> and denotes some kind of area or location; otherwise, the words have to be recognized, but should not be invented.

Examples:
Africa + -an > African
Alabama + -an > Alabaman or Alabamian (the latter preferred)
antipodes + -an > antipodean [æntɪpəʊˈdɪən]
Arizona + -an > Arizonan or Arizonian (the former preferred)
Bacon + -an > Baconian
Belgium + -an > Belgian
Christ + -an > Christian [ˈkrɪstjən]
Darwin + -an > Darwinian
Dickens + -an > Dickensian
Europe + -an > European
Italy + -an > Italian
republic + -an > republican
Russia + -an > Russian
Shakespeare + -an > Shakespearian

POTENTIAL PROBLEM: Many of the words ending in -*an* or -*ian* are nouns, either because the adjective is used as a noun as well (*Italian* can be an adjective describing, say, food, or the language spoken by Italian people) or because the word is basically a noun (*guardian, historian, librarian, musician, theologian*).

14.1.11 Other Suffixes

In this section a number of other suffixes which can be used to derive adjectives from nouns are considered. You may need to recognize these suffixes, but you should not use them to create new words. Individual words with these suffixes may be common, but the patterns as a whole are relatively limited. As a result of these factors, these affixes are for consideration by more advanced students rather than beginners.

-able: This suffix is more usually added to verbs, but is also found added to nouns as in *charitable, comfortable, knowledgeable, marriageable, merchantable, personable*.

-ary: This suffix is found on a number of relatively rare words, many of them borrowed from other languages rather than formed in English. Some examples are *dietary, hereditary, parliamentary, precautionary, reactionary, revolutionary*.

-ate: This suffix is pronounced [ɪt] when it creates adjectives from nouns, as in *fortunate, passionate*. Most often, its base is not a word of English.

-ed: This suffix can be freely attached to combinations of numeral + noun, as in *five-pointed, three-wheeled*, and is often found on combinations of adjective + noun, as in *blue-eyed, broken-hearted, quick-witted, red-handed*. It has a wider use in words like *bearded, coloured, fevered*, but these words are best learnt as individual expressions.

-en: This suffix creates adjectives meaning 'made of ~' from nouns, as in *earthen, golden, silken, wooden, woollen* (US: *woolen*). Sometimes the adjective means 'having the colouring of ~', as in *ashen, oaten*. These adjectives are often used figuratively, as in *flaxen hair, golden girl, silken voice*, with attributive use of the noun covering many of the literal meanings: *a gold ring, a silk dress*, but *a wooden bowl* as well as *a wooden expression*.

-ive: This suffix is more common on verbs than on nouns, but is also found on nominal bases. In many cases the base cannot be recognized, and extra letters may be added before the suffix. Examples include *agentive, effective, qualitative, quantitative, sensitive*.

-ly: This suffix is used mainly on bases which denote people, but there are some frequent words which do not follow this pattern. Examples include *daily, friendly, matronly, monthly, scholarly, stately, woolly*. Note that *matronly*, used to describe a woman, usually means 'plump and middle-aged'.

-ous: This suffix makes fairly formal adjectives mostly from borrowed words. When it occurs before *-ity* it sometimes takes the form *-os* (as in *porous > porosity*). Examples include *advantageous, continuous, dangerous, furious, glorious, libellous, monogamous, ruinous, vicarious, villainous*.

-some: This is a rather rare suffix, appearing in old-fashioned words, but easily recognizable. Examples include *adventuresome, awesome* ('extremely good'), *fearsome* ('to be feared'), *toothsome* ('tasty', often figurative), *troublesome* ('causing trouble').

14.2   Adjectives from Verbs

14.2.1   *The Suffix* -able

The suffix *-able* can be added freely to transitive verbs to create adjectives which mean, generally speaking, 'capable of being ~ed', where the swung dash represents the verb in the base. For example, *determinable* means 'capable of being determined'. There is a version of this suffix, *-ible*, which occurs mainly on more learned or foreign bases, but the rules for the use of the two are not entirely fixed, and sometimes both can be found with the same base: *discernable* and *discernible* are both found. If using the suffix to create a new word, use the form *-able*. Use *-ible* only when you recognize it as being the usual form. The suffix *-ate* is sometimes deleted before *-able* is added. Note that spelling rules S3 and S4 are used variably before *-able*.

Examples:
access + -ible > accessible
accept + -able > acceptable
allow + -able > allowable
alter + -able > alterable
calculate + -able > calculable
convert + -ible > convertible
deny + -able > deniable
describe + -able > describable
disperse + -ible > dispersible
educate + -able > educable
like + -able > likable
mend + -able > mendable
predict + -able > predictable
regret + -able > regrettable
replace + -able > replaceable
repress + -ible > repressible
sink + -able > sinkable

Many of the words with *-able* or *-ible* are found with negative prefixes, then meaning 'not able to be ~ed'. For example *irrepressible* means 'not able to be repressed' and *unprintable* means 'not able to be printed' (usually because too vulgar). Some of these adjectives have slightly restricted uses or meanings.

Examples:
changeable	(of weather) 'liable to change rapidly'
dependable	'that can be depended on'
impregnable	(of a fortress) 'unable to be taken by an enemy'
inedible	'not able to be eaten because of its nature'
moveable	in the phrase *moveable feast*, one not on a set day of the year, as with Easter (also used figuratively)
notable	'important'
notifiable	usually used of serious disease
operable	used mainly of cancer
opposable	used mainly of the human thumb
palpable	(of lies) 'easily discovered' (high style)
payable	'must be paid'
remarkable	'very good'
reputable	'having a good reputation'

ropeable or ropable   'extremely angry'
suitable   'appropriate'
uneatable   'not able to be eaten because it has been badly
                       prepared or has gone bad'
variable   'subject to variation'

Most words with -*able* retain the stress of the base, but a few show stress-shift.

Examples:

Word	*Normative pronunciation*	*Alternative pronunciation*
admirable	[ˈædmɪrəbl]	
analysable	[ˈænəlaɪzəbl]	[ænəˈlaɪzəbl]
applicable	[ˈæplɪkəbl]	[əˈplɪkəbl]
certifiable	[sɜːtiˈfaɪəbl]	[ˈsɜːtifaɪəbl]
comparable	[ˈkɒmpərəbl]	[kəmˈpærəbl], [kəmˈpeərəbl]
disputable	[ˈdɪspjuːtəbl]	[dɪsˈpjuːtəbl]
formidable	[ˈfɔːmɪdəbl]	[fɔːˈmɪdəbl]
lamentable	[ˈlæməntəbl]	[ləˈmentəbl]
preferable	[ˈprefərəbl]	[priˈfɜːrəbl]
revocable	[ˈrevəkəbl]	[riˈvəʊkəbl]

> ADVICE: Where available, use the regular forms of these words; the forms with stress on the first syllable may sound pedantic.

14.2.2 The Suffix -ing

Words with the suffix -*ing* (see Chapter 8) are often used as adjectives. Some of these words are completely adjectival, others are not. For example, *interesting* can be compared (*very interesting*, *more interesting*) and can be made into an adverb (*interestingly*), *cooling* is less likely to be used this way, but can be (*a very cooling breeze*), but *reading* is unlikely to be used in these ways. This means that although you can be sure that a relevant form exists, you cannot be sure, except through experience, of its precise usage.

> POTENTIAL PROBLEM: Because forms in -*ing* can be used both as nouns and as adjectives, and because both can be used before another noun, you have to be careful in understanding and reading an expression such as *shooting star* and *shooting gallery*. A *shooting star* is a star which is shooting across the sky, *shooting* is an adjective, and *shooting star* is stressed on the *star*.

A *shooting gallery* is a gallery for shooting, *shooting* is a noun, and *shooting gallery* is stressed on the *shoot-*. Very occasionally, the same written words can be interpreted either way. The expression *shooting pain* is stressed on *pain* if it means 'a pain which shoots down a limb', but is stressed on *shoot-* if it means 'a pain from having been shot'.

14.2.3 The Suffix -y

The suffix *-y* is added to a few verbs to make adjectives meaning 'having the quality of ~ing'. *Scary* means 'having the quality of scaring'. You should only use forms like this that you have already heard.

Examples:
droop + -y > droopy
flirt + -y > flirty
scare + -y > scary
sleep + -y > sleepy
squash + -y > squashy

In some cases words constructed in this way have unpredictable meanings.

Examples:
choose + -y > choosy   'difficult to please'
show + -y > showy   'ostentatious'

14.2.4 The Suffix -ish

The suffix *-ish* makes a few adjectives from verbs. You should only use words on this pattern if you have already heard them.

Examples:
tickle + -ish > ticklish
peeve + -ish > peevish

14.2.5 Other Suffixes

There are some other affixes which make adjectives from verbs, but the words they make are often very rare, the patterns are not easily perceived, and it is not easy to extend most of the patterns.

-ant: The suffix *-ant* makes nouns as well as adjectives from verbs, and the same form may share both purposes. The words thus formed are fairly formal words, and new words cannot be formed on this pattern. In many cases, the bases cannot be recognized in modern English. Examples of words that are used as adjectives include *combinant, expectant, observant, pleasant* ['plezənt], *reliant, resistant, resultant, tolerant.* Note that *expectant* most commonly collocates with *mother/parent/woman* ('expecting a child'), though it can also be used with nouns such as *audience, expression, silence* ('waiting for something to happen').

-ful: There are a few words with the suffix *-ful* added to verbs, but not particularly many, and the set cannot be easily extended. Many of the words on this pattern are now old-fashioned. Examples of current words include *heedful, resentful, vengeful, wasteful, watchful.*

-ive: The preferred pattern for the suffix *-ive* is to be added to verbs, and there are many examples. The words tend to be fairly formal, and you should not attempt to make up new words on this pattern. Some of the words using this pattern have unpredictable elements in their form or meaning. Examples include *active, assertive, demonstrative, exclusive, generative, interpretive, intuitive, inventive, progressive, submissive, suggestive.*

-ory: The suffix *-ory* makes rather rare and formal words in this pattern, although the pattern itself is quite common. There are many words with formal irregularities. You are only likely to need to learn the pattern at very advanced levels. Examples include *admonitory, compensatory, congratulatory, contradictory, defamatory, discriminatory, laudatory, respiratory, transitory.*

-some: The suffix *-some* is fairly rare in this usage, and you should not invent new words on this pattern. Adjectives of this form usually mean 'being likely to ~', but there are exceptions (e.g. *worrisome* meaning 'causing worry'). Examples include *fearsome, irksome, meddlesome, quarrelsome, tiresome, troublesome, worrisome.*

14.3   Adjectives from other Adjectives

14.3.1   The Suffix -ish

The suffix *-ish* is attached to adjectives to make new adjectives meaning 'rather ~, ~-like'. When attached to numbers, it means 'approximately ~'. Spelling rules S3 and S4 apply. You can invent new words for yourself on this pattern. Although basic adjectives are preferred as bases, things like *familiarish* are also found.

Examples:
large + -ish > largish
late + -ish > latish
nice + -ish > nicish
pale +-ish > palish
pink + -ish > pinkish
red + -ish > reddish
rowdy + -sh > rowdyish

small + -ish > smallish
smart + -ish > smartish
strong + -ish > strongish [strɒŋɪʃ]
thirty + -ish > thirtyish
white + -ish > whitish

14.3.2   The Suffix -y

The suffix -y can be added to adjectives to make new adjectives with much the same meaning as those with the suffix -ish, especially with colour adjectives. Something which is close to green in colour can be *greeny* or *greenish*. The suffix -y is not added to words that end in the sound [i], not added to numbers, and tends to sound more childish, so that -ish is to be preferred.

Examples:
yellow + -y > yellowy
crisp + -y > crispy

14.3.3   The Suffix -ful

The suffix -ful is only rarely found in this use, and words like this have to be learnt as irregular forms.

Examples:
right + -ful > rightful
wrong + -ful > wrongful

14.3.4   Other Suffixes

Other adjective-forming suffixes attach occasionally to adjectives, but such forms are irregular and of low frequency. Examples including *complicitous, distinctive, malignant, righteous.*

15

MAKING ADVERBS

15.1 Introduction

Although there are many kinds of adverb in English, there are relatively few ways of making them by morphological means. The main one is the use of the -*ly* suffix, which will be discussed at greater length just below. The problem with this suffix is not how to use it, but when not to use it, which means the discussion in this chapter will have a rather different focus from that in other chapters. Other ways of forming adverbs are discussed after the discussion of the suffix -*ly*.

15.2 The Suffix -*ly*

15.2.1 The Basic Pattern

The suffix -*ly* regularly forms adverbs from adjectives. It can be used freely with adjectives which are not extremely common. Spelling rule S2 applies. A base-final <e> is often deleted before -*ly*, but the places where it is deleted do not seem to be predictable. A base-final <le>, especially from the suffix -*able* or -*ible*, is deleted before -*ly*, and base-final <ll> is simplified to <l> before -*ly*. Except with the word *publicly*, adjectives in -*ic* take -*ally* to make adverbs.

> Examples:
> brisk + -ly > briskly
> clear + -ly > clearly
> complete + -ly > completely
> cursory + -ly> cursorily
> easy + -ly > easily
> false + -ly > falsely

final + -ly > finally
forensic + -ly > forensically
frail + -ly > frailly
full + -ly > fully
interesting + -ly > interestingly
live + -ly > lively
most + -ly > mostly
possible + -ly > possibly
presumed + -ly > presumedly [prɪˈzjuːmədli]
pretty + -ly > prettily
probable + -ly > probably
quiet + -ly > quietly
rural + -ly > rurally
slow + -ly > slowly
subtle + -ly > subtly
transparent + -ly > transparently
true + -ly > truly
truthful + -ly > truthfully
waspish + -ly > waspishly

POTENTIAL PROBLEM: There are many adjectives which also end in
-*ly* (see Section 14.1.11), so that it is not always clear what part of speech
a word ending in -*ly* belongs to. This is made much harder by the fact that
many speakers can use a lot of these -*ly* adjectives as adverbs as well. Words
like *daily, friendly, kindly, leisurely, likely* are often used either way. However,
such uses are not always universal – they may be used more in some dialects
than in others, they may be used more by younger speakers. Moreover, it is
not the case that all such words can be used as adverbs. Thus it is safer to use
such forms as adjectives only, unless you have heard them used both ways.

15.2.2 Restrictions on Using -ly

There are many instances where there is an adverb ending in -*ly* which appears
to come from a familiar adjective, but where the meaning is totally unpredictable.
Examples are given below.

hard + -ly > hardly   'very little'
late + -ly > lately   'recently'
real + -ly > really   'actually, genuinely'
rough + -ly > roughly   also means 'approximately'
scarce + -ly > scarcely   'very little'

The suffix *-ly* should not be added to adjectives which end in <ly>. We can distinguish three types of such adjectives: (i) adjectives which have a suffix *-ly* (*friendly*); (ii) adjectives which have a suffix *-y* on a base ending with <l> (*crumbly*, *scaly*); (iii) adjectives which have no suffix (*silly*). Although you will find *-ly* adverbs from some of these in dictionaries or in old texts (particularly those in group (iii)), you should not use them yourself. Twenty-first-century speakers avoid them.

There is a set of adjectives which are used to sub-modify other adjectives but are not marked as adverbs. These are intensifiers or downtoners, in this usage, and their meaning does not reflect the meaning of the adjective in isolation. Some of these are dialectal, very colloquial or even vulgar usages. Examples are given below.

> dead (intensifier) e.g. *dead interesting* 'very interesting'
> fucking (intensifier) taboo slang: do not use; e.g. *fucking stupid* 'extremely stupid'
> jolly (intensifier) now old-fashioned; e.g. *jolly silly* 'very silly'
> pretty (downtoner) e.g. *pretty depressed* 'rather depressed'
> real (intensifier) e.g. *real calm* 'very calm'

There are other cases where the adjective and the adverb share the same form, but their meanings are different. Examples are given below.

Form	Adjectival meaning	Adverbial meaning
even	'smooth, level, uniform'	'indeed, yet, in fact'
ill	'sick'	'badly'
just	'fair'	'only'
still	'quiet, peaceful'	'until now'
well	'healthy'	'in a good way'

There are many high frequency adjectives which are used as adverbs as well with no *-ly*. Some examples are given below. Some of these are found either with or without the *-ly* when used as adverbs, and the differences between the pairs vary from word to word. The use of non-*ly* adverbs of this type is more frequent in colloquial or non-standard English, and more frequent among the young.

> deep (also with -ly), fast, hard, high (also with -ly), long, loud (also with -ly), real (also with -ly), slow (also with -ly), soft (also with -ly), wrong (also with -ly)

15.3 Other Suffixes

Other suffixes used in the creation of adverbs are relatively rare and cannot be used to make new words.

-s: This is often added to phrases: *downstairs, hereabouts, overseas, sometimes, unawares*. Some of these can also be used as adjectives (as in *the downstairs cupboard*).

-ward or -wards: *backward(s), downward(s), homeward(s), onward(s), westward(s)*. The form with no *-s* can usually be used as an adjective as well; this is sometimes true of the form with an *-s*: *an upwards inflection*.

-ways: *edgeways, lengthways, sideways*. Some of these have an alternative form in *-wise* (e.g. *edgewise*).

-wise: There are two distinct meanings for this affix. The first is 'in the manner of', or 'in relation to', as in *clockwise, contrariwise, crabwise, likewise, moneywise*. The second is 'from the point of view of ~', as in *businesswise, engineeringwise, fashionwise, profitwise*. A few words may be ambiguous between having the suffix *-wise* and being a compound ending in *wise*. *Streetwise* is a compound, and means 'wise about surviving on the streets'. *Pricewise* could mean 'wise about prices' (a compound) or 'from the point of view of prices', as in *Pricewise, it would be better to shop at the other supermarket*.

There is also a prefix *a-*, creating adverbs. Examples are *abed, abeam, abroad, afield, afire, afresh, ahead, alike, alive, apart, ashore, aside, asleep*. New words on this pattern are rare, and usually poetic. Although you may need to recognize them, you should not try to invent new ones. Some of these can also be used as adjectives, but adjectives which cannot appear before the noun, only in predicate position: *★the asleep child*, but *the child is asleep*. This pattern arises historically because the *a-* is derived from a preposition, usually *on*, and a prepositional phrase cannot be used to modify a noun: *★the on-board sailor*.

16
MAKING WORDS WITH PREFIXES

For the purposes of the chapter, prefixes are classified according to the kind of information they provide: negation, location, size and so on. Within each of these major classifications, information on the kinds of bases that prefixes can be attached to is provided.

16.1 Negation

There are three common negating prefixes, and then some other rarer ones. Most of these attach to adjectives, but some can also attach to bases of other word-classes. For the creation of verbs from nouns and adjectives using some of the negative prefixes, see the chapter on making verbs (Section 13.2).

Negative prefixes make words which mean the opposite of their base. The term 'opposite', though, covers a number of different meanings. We first set out some of these different meanings.

A negative prefix can set up a scale, with the base at one end and the prefixed form at the other. This is true for a pair like *likely* and *unlikely*. There is a scale of degrees of likelihood. We term this the 'scalar' reading.

There is another reading where anything that is not-X is X. This is true for the pair *attached* and *unattached*. There are no degrees of attachment. We call this a 'contradictory' reading.

There is another reading where the opposite indicates the irrelevance of the term in the base. If something is *amoral*, it is not so much that there is a scale of morality, but that it is outside a scale of morality. We term this the 'irrelevancy' reading.

There is an opposite which indicates the undoing or reversing of an action. To *undo* something reverses the action of *doing* it. We term this the 'reversative' reading.

There is an opposite which means to remove something: to *debug* a computer is to remove the *bugs*. We call this the 'privative' reading.

There is an opposite where the base is not negated as such, but the derived form says that the action of the base is badly or poorly done. To *misuse* something is to *use* it badly. We call this the 'pejorative' reading.

Finally, there is an opposite which denies that what is denoted by the derivative is a full member of the set denoted by the base. A *non-book* is a book, but it does not have all the qualities that we expect a book to have (perhaps it has no text in it). We term this the 'atypical' reading.

16.1.1   The Prefix un-

This is the most common of the negative prefixes, and the one which it is easiest to use. In writing, it has only a single form, though the [n] may be pronounced as [m] or [ŋ] before labials or velars respectively, e.g. in *unpopular* or *unkind*. The meaning of an adjective with *un-* is usually scalar. This means that colour adjectives, which do not have another end to the scale, are rarely used with this prefix. If adjectives like *unkind* are used in the comparative, the implication is that we already know that someone/something can be classified as *unkind*, and we are considering where on the scale they fit. The un-prefixed adjective makes no such presupposition. If you ask *How kind is your aunt?* there is no assumption that she must be at the kind end of the scale rather than the unkind end of the scale. Where there are simple adjectives which are opposites of each other (e.g. *big* and *small*, *deep* and *shallow*, *high* and *low*, *dead* and *alive*) it is unusual to use *un-* on them, and preferable to use the adjective which denotes the other end of the scale, but there are cases even then when *un-* can be used. There are some adjectives, especially learned or formal adjectives, which prefer a different negative prefix, but otherwise *un-* is a fairly safe prefix to use.

Examples:
un- + able > unable
un- + alike > unalike
un- + common > uncommon
un- + friendly > unfriendly
un- + fussy > unfussy (esp. of things) 'without unnecessary extras'
un- + gentlemanly > ungentlemanly
un- + happy > unhappy
un- + kind > unkind
un- + lawful > unlawful
un- + like > unlike
un- + natural > unnatural
un- + popular > unpopular
un- + successful > unsuccessful
un- + theatrical > untheatrical

In some cases, *un-* can be attached to nouns. In these cases, *un-* has a contradictory or atypical reading. So an *unbirthday* is any day that is not your birthday. An *unperson* is a person who for some reason is lacking some quality which would allow them to be fully classified as a person. Most such words are rare, and are invented by journalists to make their prose more colourful. They are probably best avoided. Some relatively common examples are provided below.

Examples:
un- + birthday > unbirthday (usually joking)
un- + belief > unbelief ('lack of religious faith')
un- + repair > unrepair (also, more commonly, *disrepair*)

Most words that look as though they might have *un-* prefixed to a noun, actually have *un* prefixed to an adjective, and the complex adjective then turned into a noun. That is, *uncertainty* should be seen as *[uncertain]ty* rather than as *un[certainty]*.

When *un-* is added to verbs it usually has a reversative or privative meaning. The privative reading is found where the base might be a noun or a verb.

Examples:
un- + bar > unbar
un- + bind > unbind
un- + buckle > unbuckle
un- + furl > unfurl
un- + install > uninstall
un- + learn > unlearn
un- + tie > untie

Because *un-* can attach to adjectives (which may include past participles) with one meaning, and to verbs with another, a sequence of *un-* followed by a past participle can be ambiguous. The word *undivided* means 'not divided' so the *un-* is added to the adjective; the word *unfettered* means 'let loose from chains' and so the *un-* is added to the noun *fetter*. The first of these two possibilities is the more common one. This means that although *unclothed* could apparently be understood either way, we would probably prefer to read it as 'not clothed' rather than 'having had the clothes removed'.

POTENTIAL PROBLEM: There are a few adjectives with the *un-* prefix where the base has no independent existence.

Examples:
uncouth
unkempt

16.1.2   *The Prefix* in-

There are four variants of this prefix in the written form: *in-* occurs when none of the others is necessary, *im-* occurs before bilabial consonants, *il-* occurs before <l> and *ir-* occurs before <r>. In pronunciation, the last two are both pronounced [ɪ]. This prefix is added to adjectives, and in many cases there is an *in-* at the beginning of negative adjectives, even though the base is not recognizable and cannot stand alone. The meaning of *in-* is just the same as the meaning of *un-* on adjectives, discussed above. The prefix *in-* is added to learned adjectives, so there are few two-syllable adjectives with the prefix *in-* (*insane* is one, and *inept* and *inert* show cases where the base is not recognizable).

Examples:
in- + accurate > inaccurate
in- + correct > incorrect
in- + describable > indescribable
in- + dependent > independent
in- + formal > informal
in- + frequent > infrequent
in- + hospitable > inhospitable
in- + legal > illegal
in- + literate > illiterate
in- + numerate > innumerate
in- + possible > impossible
in- + relevant > irrelevant
in- + regular > irregular

In a few instances, the stress falls on the *in-* prefix.

Examples:
in- + pious > impious ['ɪmpɪəs]
in- + famous > infamous ['ɪnfəməs] 'notorious'
in- + potent > impotent ['ɪmpətənt]

> NOTE: *impertinent* means 'cheeky', while *pertinent* means 'relevant'. *Improper* negates *proper* 'seemly' and never *proper* 'actual, real'. *Inorganic* negates *organic* meaning 'derived from living material' and never *organic* 'grown without artificial aids'.

Sometimes there is variation between the prefix *in-* and the prefix *un-*. Sometimes these mean the same thing ('=' in the examples below), sometimes they do not ('≠' in the examples below). Sometimes these pairs have different but nearly synonymous bases, sometimes the same. Note that the noun that goes with *unjust* is *injustice*.

inedible	≠	uneatable	a stone is inedible, but food that has been burnt might be uneatable
illegal	=	unlawful	
illegible	≠	unreadable	writing is illegible when you cannot make out the letters; a document is unreadable because its style is bad or because it is boring
inorganic	≠	unorganic	inorganic is used of e.g. stones as opposed to plants which are organic; unorganic means 'grown with chemical fertilizers and/or insect sprays'
innavigable	=	unnavigable	
insensitive	=	unsensitive	
insensible	≠	unsensible	unsensible means 'not sensible'; insensible means 'having lost consciousness'
invaluable	≠	unvaluable	*unvaluable* means 'having no value'; *invaluable* means 'being so precious that one cannot assign a value to it'

The prefix *in-* is sometimes found on nouns, but usually with the sense of 'the quality of not being ~', where the missing part of the meaning is adjectival: *inefficiency* means 'the quality of not being efficient'.

16.1.3 *The Prefix* non-

In writing, the prefix *non-* always has the same form; in pronunciation there may be some assimilation of the final [n] to the place of articulation of the next consonant. The prefix *non-* creates contradictory negatives. For example, a *non-accidental injury* is any injury that does not occur through an accident; a *non-alcoholic drink* is any drink that does not contain alcohol (tea, coffee, fruit juice, milk, soft drinks); a *non-smoker* is a person who does not smoke. Sometimes, when added to nouns, *non-* has an atypical reading: a *non-person* is a person who, for example, because they have no passport, does not qualify for citizenship or who is otherwise considered to be a nonentity.

Examples:

With adjective bases

non- + custodial > non-custodial (of a sentence in a court, 'not involving time in prison')

non- + existent > non-existent

non- + metallic > non-metallic ('made of something other than metal')

non- + negative > non-negative (mathematics, of a number: 'positive or zero')

non- + verbal > nonverbal (of communication, 'not using spoken words; using gesture or sign, or facial expression')

With noun base

non- + combatant > non-combatant ('person who is not a soldier in an army')

non- + event > non-event ('event of no significance')

non- + fiction > nonfiction ('factual writing')

non- + issue > non-issue ('issue not worthy of discussion')

non- + starter > nonstarter ('a horse that does not run a race; anything with no chance of success')

There are also some adjectives made with the prefix *non-* and a verbal base. Examples are *non-drip* ('which does not drip when washed'), *non-stick* ('which does not allow food to stick to it during cooking'), *non-stop* ('direct, without intermediate stops').

Because of its meaning, *non-* can contrast with *un-* or *in-*. For example, the word *un-Christian* is used of behaviour (etc.) which is considered to be contrary to the teachings of the Christian church, while *non-Christian* means 'not belonging to the Christian religion'. However, in many cases the distinction between *un-* and *non-* (for instance) is so small that the prefixes can be used interchangeably: *non-rational* and *unrational* (or *irrational*) may mean more or less the same thing.

16.1.4   The prefix a-

The prefix *a-* has the form *an-* when it occurs before a vowel, and often before an <h>. The prefix is of Greek origin, and still attaches preferably to words of Greek origin. The result is that it is used only in technical and learned words. Sometimes alternative negative prefixes can be used without changing the meaning. In a few cases, there is a meaning change. When this occurs, the prefix *a-* has a contradictory or irrelevant reading, while the alternative affix has a scalar reading.

Examples:

a- + historical > ahistorical 'not in accordance with history'

a- + hydrous > anhydrous 'not containing water'

a- + moral > amoral ('not having any morals'; *immoral* means 'going against moral precepts')

a- + oestrous > anoestrous

a- + political > apolitical

a- + semantic > asemantic 'having no meaning'

a- + sexual > asexual (e.g. of reproduction) 'not by sexual means'

a- + typical > atypical (also *untypical*)

16.1.5   The prefixes de- and dis-

These two prefixes can be added to verbs. When added to verbs they usually have reversative meaning. *Dis-* can also be added to nouns.

Examples:

On nouns

dis- + belief > disbelief

dis- + comfort > discomfort

dis- + honour > dishonour

dis- + respect > disrespect

dis- + taste > distaste

On verbs

de- + centralize > decentralize

de- + compose > decompose 'rot'

de- + compress > decompress

de- + hydrate > dehydrate 'lose water, remove water from'

de- + odorize > deodorize

de- + populate > depopulate 'empty of people'

dis- + appear > disappear 'vanish'

dis- + assemble > disassemble 'take apart'

dis- + connect > disconnect 'separate from'

dis- + inter > disinter 'dig up'

dis- + prove > disprove

dis- + trust > distrust

16.1.6   The prefixes mal- and mis-

These prefixes usually have a pejorative meaning. They are both used on nouns and verbs, but many of the nouns come from the verbs. *Mis-* is sometimes used on the past participles of verbs. These prefixes are rather rarer than some of the others, but are still used for new words, but because of their relative rarity it is not recommended to invent new words with them.

Examples on verbs:

mal- + align > malalign

mal- + function > malfunction

mal- + nourish > malnourish

mal- + treat > maltreat

mis- + deal > misdeal (in a card game)

mis- + file > misfile

mis- + inform > misinform

mis- + judge > misjudge

mis- + manage > mismanage

mis- + use > misuse

NOTE: The negative prefix *ig-* appears only in the form *ignoble*, the opposite of *noble*.

The prefix *ab-* in *abuse* and *abnormal*, although it comes from a Latin form meaning 'away from', functions much like *mis-* as a pejorative prefix.

16.2 Location

Most prefixes that show location in space can also show location in time. For example, *pre-* can mean 'further forward than' in words like *pre-cortex*, and can mean 'at an earlier time' in *preapprove*.

There are many of these prefixes, because there is very often a native prefix (which sometimes looks just like a preposition) and a learned one (often historically from French or Latin, sometimes both), and they may be more or less synonymous. Because there are so many, some of the rarer ones are omitted here.

Where prefixes look like prepositions, the analysis can be difficult. Such problems are ignored here, since it does not matter much whether the *in-* in *ingrown* is a word (and *ingrown* is a compound) or a prefix (so *ingrown* is a derivative). In principle, similar problems exist for the learned forms. Many of these exist as prefixes in English, attached to things which are words in English; many are attached to words from French or Latin or Greek and were prepositions in historical times, but today do not have bases which are English words.

Most of these forms can be found attached to nouns, verbs or adjectives, as appropriate. No attempt will be made to illustrate all possible patterns.

16.2.1 In Front of, Earlier in Time: The Prefixes fore-, pre- and ante-

The prefix *fore-* is added most freely to nouns, but also to verbs. It is used for time and place. The prefix *pre-* is used particularly for time, but also for place. Its use for place is particularly in scientific contexts. It can attach to nouns, verbs and adjectives. It is often found in words that are borrowed from Latin, where the base may not be recognizable (e.g. *precede, preclude, prevent*). *Ante-* is the rarest of the three prefixes. It can attach to nouns, verbs or adjectives, but is rarely found on verbs. It usually denotes space on nouns and time on adjectives, but that may not be systematic.

Examples:
fore- + tell > foretell (= predict)
fore- + shore > foreshore
fore- + arm > forearm (noun, 'part of the arm', with stress on the first syllable; verb, 'arm in advance', with stress on the second syllable)
fore- + head > forehead (traditionally ['fɒrɪd], now usually ['fɔːhed])
fore- + see > foresee
fore- + name > forename
fore- + warn > forewarn
pre- + adolescent > preadolescent
pre- + heat > preheat
pre- + war > pre-war (adjective or adverb)
pre- + cut > precut (verb or adjective)
pre- + natal > prenatal (= antenatal)
pre- + maxilla > premaxilla
pre- + school > pre-school (noun or verb)
pre- + view > preview
ante- + chamber > antechamber
ante- + room > anteroom
ante- + natal > antenatal (= prenatal)
ante- + date > antedate (verb)

16.2.2   Behind, After in Time: The Prefixes **after-, back-, post-, retro-**

The prefix *after-* attaches mainly to nouns, and although it can be used for both time and place, it is more often used for time. When attached to verbs, *back-* often means to perform the action in reverse. Attached to nouns, it sometimes means 'at a distance from the centre of attention', but can also mean 'behind' in location. It is not used for time. *Post-* is usually used for time, but is sometimes used for location. It attaches primarily to adjectives, but is also found on nouns and verbs. *Retro-* is a rare prefix, found on nouns, verbs and adjectives. It most often means 'backwards'. It is also found in borrowed words, where the base is unrecognizable (e.g. *retrocede, retrospect*). There is also a word *retro*, which comes from the prefix, which means 'mimicking the fashion of past times', and this can often be used in compounds like *retro-chic*, where it might look like the prefix. It is now more common than the prefix.

Examples:

after- + noon > afternoon

after- + birth > afterbirth ('placenta', delivered after the birth of the baby)

after- + taste > aftertaste

after- + deck > afterdeck

back- + fire > backfire (noun or verb)

back- + comb > backcomb (verb)

back- + formation > backformation

back- + cloth > backcloth

back- + woods > backwoods

back- + slide > backslide (verb)

back- + pedal > backpedal (verb)

back- + street > backstreet

post- + date > postdate (verb; opposite of predate or antedate)

post- + adolescent > postadolescent

post- + doctoral > postdoctoral

post- + impressionism > Post-impressionism

post- + modern > post-modern

post- + orbital > postorbital

post- + vocalic > postvocalic ('following a vowel')

post- + war > post-war (adjective or adverb)

retro- + active > retroactive

retro- + fit > retrofit

retro- + flex > retroflex

retro- + rocket > retrorocket

16.2.3   Under in Space: The Prefixes sub-, under-

The prefix *sub-* is added to nouns, verbs and adjectives. It can mean literally 'underneath', but can also mean 'inferior to, of lesser status'. This second meaning is also found where it refers to an inferior level of classification. Similar meanings are found with *under-*.

Examples:

sub- + marine > submarine (adjective, from that, a noun)

sub- + liminal > subliminal

sub- + committee > sub-committee

sub- + culture > sub-culture

sub- + group > subgroup

sub- + lease > sublease (verb or noun)

sub- + lieutenant > sub-lieutenant

sub- + human > subhuman

sub- + normal > subnormal
under- + class > underclass
under- + coat > undercoat
under- + cook > undercook (noun, 'person who answers to the head cook' and verb 'not cook quite enough')
under- + belly > underbelly (usu. figurative)
under- + perform > underperform
under- + state > understate (verb)
under- + growth > undergrowth ('plants growing under trees in a wooded area')
under- + lip > underlip (also bottom lip)
under- + world > underworld
under- + paid > underpaid

16.2.4   Above in Space: The Prefixes sur-, super-, over-

The prefix *sur-* is rare, and is often used to mean 'to a greater extent, more than'. The prefix *super-* often has the same meaning, and this is linked to its most usual meaning of 'particularly large or fine' (for which see below, Section 16.3.2). In many instances, *super-* is found on bases which are not English words (e.g. *supersede*, *supervise*).

Examples:
sur- + charge > surcharge
sur- + pass > surpass
sur- + real > surreal
super- + tax > supertax
super- + sonic > supersonic
super- + human > superhuman
super- + charge > supercharge
super- + impose > superimpose
super- + natural > supernatural
over- + achieve > overachieve
over- + act > overact
over- + confident > overconfident
over- + look > overlook (often 'to fail to take into account')
over- + hang > overhang
over- + flow > overflow (verb and noun)
over- + elaborate > overelaborate (adjective)
over- + draught > overdraught ('amount of money taken from an account exceeding the funds held there') (US: overdraft)
over- + lord > overlord

16.2.5 Around: The Prefixes circum- and peri-

Both of these prefixes are most frequently attached to bases which are not English words (e.g. *circumspect, circumscribe, perihelion, peripatetic, peristalsis*). With *circum-*, this is particularly the case with verbs, most of which have bases which are not English words. With *peri-*, most of the words which use it have such a form. *Circum-* appears to be used most in spatial senses, while *peri-* can be either spatial or temporal.

Examples:
circum- + lunar > circumlunar
circum- + navigate > circumnavigate
circum- + polar > circumpolar
circum- + solar > circumsolar
peri- + natal > perinatal
peri- + glacial > periglacial

16.2.6 Previously in Time: The Prefix ex-

This prefix is added only to nouns, to denote something which once had a status and no longer has. There is a different prefix *ex-*, meaning 'out of, outside', which is most often used with bases that are not English words (see Section 16.2.7).

Examples:
ex- + addict > ex-addict
ex- + husband > ex-husband
ex- + wife > ex-wife

16.2.7 Outside, Moving Away From: The Prefixes ex-, out-

The prefix *ex-* is usually used on bases which are not English words (e.g. *expel, expire, explore*). The prefix *extra-* is usually added to adjectives when the base is an English word. It usually means 'beyond'. The prefix *out-* is usually added to verbs, to mean 'to perform the action of the verb in such a way as to beat someone else'. On nouns, *out-* may have a literal spatial meaning.

Examples:
ex- + communicate > excommunicate ('ban from communion in the church')
ex- + directory > ex-directory (adjective, 'not in the telephone directory')
ex- + patriate > expatriate ('person living outside their native country')
out- + building > outbuilding ('a building away from the main building')
out- + class > outclass (verb)
out- + do > outdo

out- + field > outfield ('the most distant part of a sports field')
out- + grow > outgrow ('to grow too big for the conditions')
out- + patient > outpatient ('patient not resident in the hospital')
out- + stare > outstare
out- + let > outlet (noun, 'a place for surplus to escape; a shop')

16.2.8   Across: The Prefix trans-

The prefix *trans-* is most often used on bases that are not English words (e.g. *transfer, transpire*). It means 'across; from across; through; and occasionally, beyond'.

Examples:
trans- + Atlantic > trans-Atlantic
trans- + alpine > transalpine
trans- + fix > transfix (verb, 'pierce' – often figuratively)
trans- + form > transform (verb, 'change radically')
trans- + plant > transplant (verb or noun)
trans- + ship > transship (verb, 'move from one form of transport to another')
trans- + uranic > transuranic ('having an atomic number beyond that of uranium')

16.2.9   Between: The Prefix inter-

The prefix *inter-* is often used with a base that is not an English word (e.g. *interrupt, intervene*). It means 'between; reciprocal'.

Examples:
inter- + act > interact
inter- + dental > interdental
inter- + face > interface
inter- + faith > interfaith (adjective)
inter- + galactic > intergalactic
inter- + mingle > intermingle
inter- + national > international
inter- + racial > interracial
inter- + view > interview ('meeting involving question and answer')

16.2.10   Inside and Outside: The Prefixes intra-, extra-, endo- and exo-

The prefix *intra-* is used mostly on adjectives, and means 'within, inside'. It is usually added to very learned words, and thus forms very learned words. The prefix *extra-* is the corresponding prefix meaning 'outside, external'. The prefix *endo-* is mostly added to bases which are not English words. It means 'internal, within'. It is mostly used in scientific vocabulary. The prefix *exo-* is the corresponding prefix meaning 'external, outside'.

Examples:
endo- + skeleton > endoskeleton
endo- + thermic > endothermic ('warm-blooded')
exo- + skeleton > exoskeleton
exo- + biology > exobiology ('the study of non-terrestrial life')
extra- + corporeal > extracorporeal
extra- + galactic > extragalactic
extra- + mural > extramural (usu. 'outside the [walls of the] institution')
extra- + ordinary > extraordinary [ɪkˈstrɔːdɪnəri]
extra- + sensory > extrasensory ('beyond the reach of the five senses')
extra- + curricular > extracurricular
extra- + territorial > extraterritorial
intra- + mural > intramural ('within [the walls of] the institution')
intra- + net > intranet
intra- + uterine > intrauterine
intra- + venous > intravenous [ɪnˈtrævənəs] ('inside a vein; directly into a vein')

16.2.11   For and Against: The Prefixes pro-, anti-, contra- and counter-

The prefix *pro-* is used mainly on bases that are not English words (e.g. *propel, protect*). The only meaning in which it can be used to make new words is when it means 'in favour of ~', and contrasts with *anti-*. It is used occasionally with other meanings such as 'replacement ~' or 'in front of ~'. The prefix *anti-* is used to make new words meaning 'having an attitude opposed to ~'. It is also used in scientific and medical contexts to mean 'something used to counteract the effects of ~'. The prefix *contra-* is a rare prefix which, in music, can mean 'pitched lower than ~' and in a spatial sense can mean 'moving in the opposite direction from the ~'. It is most often used with a base which is not an English word (e.g. *contraception, contradict*). The prefix *counter-* is used to mean 'in opposition to ~' so that a *counterclaim* is a claim in opposition to another claim.

Examples:
anti- + acid > antiacid or antacid
anti- + British > anti-British
anti- + freeze > antifreeze ('fluid used to prevent the water in a car's radiator from freezing')

anti- + fungal > antifungal ('preparation used to counteract fungus')
anti- + government > antigovernment (adjective)
anti- + lock > anti-lock (of vehicle brakes) ('designed to prevent the wheels from locking, to minimize skid')
anti- + racism > anti-racism
anti- + social > antisocial
contra- + bass > contrabass ('instrument pitched lower than a bass')
contra- + flow > contraflow ('vehicles travelling counter to the usual direction of travel on a motorway, when vehicles going in both directions share a lane')
counter- + act > counteract
counter- + attack > counterattack
counter- + bid > counterbid (noun or verb)
counter- + factual > counterfactual
counter- + irritant > counter-irritant
counter- + proposal > counter-proposal
counter- + productive > counterproductive
counter- + revolution > counter-revolution
counter- + weight > counterweight
pro- + clitic > proclitic
pro- + British > pro-British
pro- + consul > proconsul
pro- + marketeer > pro-marketeer

16.2.12   Together: The Prefix co-

The prefix *co-* is used on nouns and verbs (and occasionally on adjectives) to mean 'together'. It can be viewed as an English version of *con-* (sometimes *com-*, *col-* or *cor-*) which is the Latin form.

Examples:
co- + axial > co-axial
co- + defendant > co-defendant
co- + exist > co-exist
co- + extensive > co-extensive
co- + respondent > co-respondent (a *co-respondent* is a man or woman charged with adultery, as opposed to a *correspondent*, who is someone who writes to you)
co- + signatory > co-signatory
co- + star > co-star (noun or verb)
co- + worker > co-worker

16.2.13   In the Middle: The Prefix mid-

This prefix means 'in the middle of' or 'half-way through'. It can be used both for place and for time.

Examples:
mid- + Cambrian > mid-Cambrian
mid- + channel > midchannel
mid- + field > midfield
mid- + night > midnight
mid- + stream > mid-stream
mid- + Victorian > mid-Victorian
mid- + winter > midwinter

16.3   Size

A number of prefixes show relative size, usually something that is smaller than the norm or something that is larger than the norm. For suffixes which are used to denote small things, see Section 16.3.1. Many of these prefixes have precise scientific meanings, and rather loose everyday meanings. Some of the prefixes that show large size are used in isolation as words to indicate approval or high quality (e.g. *mega*, *super*). Others have wider use as nouns or adjectives (e.g. *mini*, *hyper*).

16.3.1   Small Size: The Prefixes mini-, nano-, micro-

The prefix *mini-* is originally an abbreviation of *miniature*, and it has that basic meaning. In technical usage, *nano-* means '10^{-9}'; in non-scientific usage it means 'microscopically small'. In technical usage, *micro-* means '10^{-6}'; in ordinary usage it means 'microscopically small'.

Examples:
micro- + film > microfilm
micro- + bar > microbar
micro- + brewery > microbrewery ('small scale brewery')
micro- + cassette > microcassette
micro- + computer > microcomputer
micro- + mesh > micromesh
micro- + wave > microwave
mini- + bike > minibike
mini- + break > minibreak ('short holiday')
mini- + cab > minicab ('unlicensed taxi')
mini- + disc (US disk) > minidisc
mini- + ski > miniski

nano- + metre > nanometre
nano- + technology > nanotechnology
nano- + tube > nanotube

16.3.2 Large Size: The Prefixes maxi-, super-, hyper-, uber-, macro, mega- and ultra-

The prefix *maxi-* is now rare, and was mostly used as a fashion term to indicate full length. The prefix *super-* has already been mentioned (Section 16.2.4) in its spatial sense. In the words considered here it means 'large; particularly fine; excessive'. It is used both technically and in colloquial language. The prefix *hyper-* usually indicates an excessive degree, especially in medical terminology. It is often used with a base that is not an English word (e.g. *hyperbole, hypernym, hypergamy*). The prefix *uber-* (also written <ueber> and <über>) is a recent borrowing from German. Attached to adjectives it means 'excessively ~', attached to nouns, it means 'an archetypical example of a ~'. *Macro-* is a relatively rare prefix, used mainly in science, and often on a base which is not an English word (e.g. *macrocosm*). It means 'large; on a large scale'. The prefix *ultra-* originally meant 'beyond', and that meaning is still found in some scientific words. More colloquially, it just means 'extremely'.

Examples:
hyper- + active > hyperactive
hyper- + inflation > hyperinflation (in economics)
hyper- + market > hypermarket (larger than a supermarket)
hyper- + sensitive > hypersensitive
hyper- + tension > hypertension ('excessively high blood pressure')
macro- + economic > macro-economic
macro- + molecule > macromolecule
macro- + fauna > macrofauna
maxi- + coat > maxicoat
maxi- + rich > maxirich
maxi- + skirt > maxiskirt
maxi- + yacht > maxiyacht
super- + charge > supercharge (verb)
super- + dense > superdense
super- + ego > superego (in Freudian psychology)
super- + fit > superfit ('extremely healthy')
super- + glue > superglue
super- + highway > superhighway
super- + market > supermarket
super- + nova > supernova
super- + sonic > supersonic
uber- + rich > uber-rich

uber- + professor > uber-professor
ultra- + left-wing > ultra-left-wing
ultra- + orthodox > ultraorthodox
ultra- + sonic > ultrasonic
ultra- + violet > ultra-violet

16.3.3   Repetition: The Prefix re-

The prefix *re-* [riː] is most often used on verbs, but is also found on corresponding nouns and adjectives. It is freely available on verbs.

Examples:
re- + cycle > recycle
re- + attach > reattach
re- + apply > re-apply
re- + build > rebuild
re- + do > redo
re- + educate > re-educate ('to change a person's beliefs')
re- + draft > redraft
re- + define > redefine
re- + draw > redraw
re- + embark > re-embark
re- + play > replay (noun or verb)

POTENTIAL PROBLEM: There is another prefix, or apparent prefix, with the form <re> which is usually pronounced [rɪ] and which is not freely available. Its meaning is often obscure, or the meaning of the words it creates is not transparent. In some cases this *re-* is added to adjectives to make verbs.

Examples:
re- + fresh > refresh
re- + new > renew
re- + lax > relax

In some cases it is in apparent contrast with the available *re-* [riː]. Note in the examples below that a hyphen is used to separate the prefix *re-* 'again' from the base so as to minimize the confusion with the unhyphenated word. This is normal usage.

Examples:

Prefix [riː]	Meaning	Prefix [rɪ]	Meaning
re-call	'call again'	recall	'remember'
re-cover	'cover again'	recover	'get better after an illness'
re-dress	'dress (someone) again'	redress	'set right'
re-lease	'grant a new lease'	release	'let go'
re-mark	'mark again'	remark	'make an observation'
re-sign	'sign again'	resign	'give up a position'

It is not clear whether this counts as the same *re-* which is often found on bases that are not English verbs (especially when forming verbs).

Examples:
recite
recur
refer
reflect
remain
remand
remit
repeal
repel

Because of these various types of initial *re-* (not to mention those instances where *re-* is clearly not a prefix, as in *realize, rectify, regular, rely*), care is needed in interpreting such words.

16.4   Numbers

There are a lot of prefixes which indicate numbers. Most of these are borrowed from Latin and Greek, and they can occur in the kind of word-formation discussed in Chapter 18. They are also found attached to English words.

Examples:

½	semi- + final > semi-final
½	semi- + skilled > semi-skilled
1	mono- + chromatic > monochromatic
1	mono- + syllable > monosyllable
1	mono- + tone > monotone
1	uni- + cellular > unicellular

1	uni- + cycle > unicycle	
2	bi- + cycle > bicycle	
2	bi- + polar > bipolar	
2	di- + syllabic > disyllabic	(also bisyllabic)
2	di- + morphism > dimorphism	
2	duo- + decimal > duodecimal	
3	tri- + cycle > tricycle	
4	quadra- + angle > quadrangle	
4	quadri- + partite > quadripartite	
4	tetra- + chloride > tetrachloride	
5	penta- + angle > pentangle	
5	quin- + centenary > quincentenary	
10	deca- + syllable > decasyllable	
10	deci- + litre > decilitre	
100	centi- + metre > centimetre	
100	hecto- + gram > hectogram	
1,000	kilo- + gram > kilogram	
1,000	milli- + litre > millilitre	
all	omni- + present > omnipresent	
all	omni- + science > omniscience	[ɒmˈnɪsɪəns] or [ɒmˈnɪʃəns]
all	pan- + American > pan-American	
many	multi- + national > multi-national	
many	poly- + crystal > polycrystal	
both	ambi- + syllabic > ambisyllabic	

17
MAKING WORDS WITHOUT AFFIXES

There are a number of patterns where new words are made without adding any affix. Sometimes some change is made to the base – a change of consonant sound, a change of vowel sound, a change of stress – sometimes no change at all is made. Most of these processes cannot be freely used to make new words, though recognizing the pattern might help interpret the relationship between the words. In some cases there are good reasons for believing that we know which of the two words came from which, but it is much safer simply to say that there is a relationship between the two without worrying about which is the original base and which is the derivative. In some cases it is not clear that we are dealing with 'new words' at all. Since this is often the case with the most reliable sets, they will be mentioned here, though they are often not seen as morphological patterns at all.

17.1 Relationships Between Words with the Same Form

The theory dealing with words like this is confused and often contradictory. Even the terminology is extremely variable. Terms like conversion, zero-derivation, functional shift and relisting are all used to describe the phenomenon, with differing theoretical implications. Here, such theoretical problems are ignored, and the patterns alone are of interest.

17.1.1 Noun and Verb

In English, it is extremely common for a noun and a verb to have the same form and to be related in meaning. This phenomenon is found with very common words, especially ones made up of a single syllable, as well as with rare ones. In some instances, it makes it difficult to know whether another affixed form has the verb or the noun as its base. For example, the word *guider* might come from the verb *guide* or from the noun *guide*; we might even argue that it comes from both, in different contexts. These words are not, in general terms, predictable, and nor is the precise meaning of the noun (the noun may have several different meanings). This means you have to learn these words individually. In the presentation of examples a distinction will be made between instances where the noun is an event and instances where the noun is a person (or instrument, etc.).

Examples with event nouns:
control
love
remark
drive
package
pressure
return
surrender
dream
summer
help
spread
kill
yawn

Examples with person or instrument nouns:
bus
chauffeur
cook
flirt
glue
guide
hammer
judge
press
spy
whisk

In some examples where there is form in common between a noun and a verb, the meaning is different enough for us to wonder whether the same relationship exists as with the kinds illustrated above or not. Often this is because of changes in meaning over a long period of time.

Examples:

Form	Noun meaning	Verb meaning
book	'bound volume'	'to order in advance'
notice	'public announcement'	'to see and remark on'
spare	'extra person or thing'	'to save'
study	also 'room in which to study'	'to learn from books'

17.1.2   Noun and Noun

Most of the examples here are usually considered to be matters of syntax, polysemy, or figurative extension. They are listed for the sake of completeness.

Countability

Although it is now commonplace to find nouns listed in dictionaries as being countable or uncountable, there is an argument that no noun is specifically countable or uncountable, all nouns can be either in a suitable context. Even a word like *bread*, which is often viewed as the uncountable congener for *loaf*, can be countable with the sense 'types of bread' and *loaf* can be uncountable in the sense 'portion of food'. Speakers can, that is to say, manipulate countability for semantic purposes. Of course, most nouns tend to be countable most of the time or uncountable most of the time. There are very few nouns that must be one or the other.

Examples:

applause	nearly always uncountable
chaos	very hard to make countable
chess	very hard to make countable
fun	nearly always uncountable
homework	very hard to make countable
information	nearly always uncountable
knowledge	very hard to make countable
research	nearly always uncountable
shopping	nearly always uncountable

Where countable and uncountable contrast with each other, there are some meanings which tend to recur with one class or the other.

Countable: 'portion of, for human consumption', 'types of', 'object made with a material', 'person or thing displaying an abstract quality', 'a limited example of a continuing activity'

Uncountable: 'type of food or drink for human consumption', 'material', 'abstract quality', 'an action or continuing activity'

Proper and Common

Names can be used as common nouns without any change of form (and without losing their capital letter in spelling). Examples (invented) of the types of usage that demand this are shown below.

> I know three Elizabeths.
> There is a Paris in France and a Paris in Texas.
> The Patrick I'm talking about lives in London.
> Which James do you want to see?
> The Smiths are coming to dinner this evening.
> We need a second Alexander Pope.

Reasons for using names as common nouns mean that not every name is very likely in this usage, but the usage is always available.

17.1.3 Noun and Adjective

Most words that we think of as adjectives can occur with the definite article and no noun, creating a full noun phrase. Where such noun phrases denote something non-human, there is singular agreement, when they denote something human, there is plural agreement. So *the poor* in *The poor are a perpetual problem for policy makers* means 'poor people', while *the impossible* in *The impossible has a way of happening tomorrow* means 'impossible things'. Despite the easy availability of this construction, it is not always used. We would not say ⋆*The important is how you feel* but would prefer *The important thing is how you feel*. The unclear limits to such constructions mean that they should not be overused. In this construction, only the definite article is used, and the definite article must be used. No genitive marking, no post-adjectival modifying phrases are permitted.

In other cases, something which might look like an adjective has all the behaviour of a noun: it can be made plural, it can take any determiner, it can be submodified, and so on. This construction, however, is not freely available, and you have to know what words can be both adjectives and nouns. In the chapters on making adjectives (Chapter 14) and making nouns (Chapter 12), some examples have been given of affixes which can be used in both ways, but even here, not all words with the relevant affixes can be used both ways.

For example, a word like *intellectual* has an adjectival affix *-al*, but we can say *this intellectual, this well-known intellectual, intellectuals in Paris* and so on. But *emotional* does not seem to allow this construction. Some of the words that do allow full nominal behaviour denote people (like *intellectual, international*), others denote non-humans or non-animates, like *annual* (a plant or a publication), *dental* (a speech sound), but most words created with adjectival *-al* allow only an adjectival reading. The examples here have focused on the suffix *-al*, but the same is true with other suffixes. We can have a *friendly* (sporting engagement), but not a *scholarly*; we can have a *psychic* (person), but not an *organic*; we can have a *glossy* (magazine), but not a *thrifty*. Accordingly, only words which you have heard used in this way can be used in this way; you cannot assume that this construction will be possible.

17.1.4   Other Relationships

Gradability

Non-gradable adjectives can be made gradable. Examples of how such forms are used are provided below.

> She is more French than the French.
> Christchurch is said to be the most English of the cities in New Zealand.
> The atomic clock is less atomic than it sounds.

Transitivity

There are many cases of intransitive and transitive verbs with the same form. Some care is required with the distinction here. *He drinks* (meaning 'he imbibes rather more alcohol than is good for him') might be a transitive verb with the direct object deleted rather than a genuine intransitive verb. *He lives a life of ease* may be a very limited use of a verb that is not entirely transitive. But there are many standard examples, where the usage seems canonical on both sides.

Verb	*Intransitive use*	*Transitive use*
blow up	The factory blew up	The robbers blew up the factory
collapse	He collapsed in the street	He collapsed the tent
continue	The rain continued all day	I continued my quest
grow	Weeds grow in our garden	We grow tomatoes
open	The door opened silently	I opened the door
see	I can see	I saw the new movie
shrink	My trousers shrank in the wash	She shrank the cotton by washing it
smell	The rubbish smells	The dog can smell a rabbit
unite	The two societies united	She managed to unite the two societies
visit	My aunt will visit in the spring	I want to visit Beijing
walk	I walk to work regularly	I have to walk the dog

17.2 Relationships Between Words with Related but Different Form

17.2.1 Related Words with Different Vowels

There is a relatively small, fixed, set of words which are related in meaning and differ in the vowel. Examples are provided below.

abide (verb)	abode (noun)
bleed (verb)	blood (noun)
breed (verb)	brood (noun)
fall (intransitive)	fell (transitive, causative)
feed (verb)	food (noun)
fill (verb)	full (adjective)
lie (intransitive)	lay (transitive)
rise (intransitive)	raise (transitive)
shoot (verb)	shot (noun)
sing (verb)	song (noun)
sit (intransitive)	set (transitive)

Much more common is the situation where related words, related by morphology or just by meaning, have different vowels in the root.

broad	breadth
cat	kitten
clear	clarity
cone	conic(al)
deep	depth
fool	folly
ghost	ghastly
goose	gosling
long	length
pronounce	pronunciation
sane	sanity
see	sight
shade	shadow
wide	width

The limits of this phenomenon are hard to draw, since relatedness of meaning lies in the eye of the beholder. Some might see *moon* and *month* as related, or *heal* and *health*, others would not. Examples like these should not be taken particularly seriously, because they do not seem, in general, to predict other forms.

Change in vowel quality also affects some words where there is a change of consonant and, especially, where there is a change of stress. Such examples are examined below.

17.2.2 *Related Words with Different Consonants*

There is a series of related nouns and verbs which end in fricative consonants. This is a finite list, though there are some words which are now rarely used which belong on the list. No new words can be added to the list. The most relevant pairs are listed below

Noun	*Verb*
belief	believe
calf	calve 'give birth to a calf'
grief	grieve
half	halve
house [haʊs]	house [haʊz]
mouth [maʊθ]	mouth [maʊð]
proof [pruːf]	prove [pruːv]
relief	relieve
sheaf	sheave
sheath [ʃiːθ]	sheathe [ʃiːð]
shelf	shelve 'put on a shelf'
strife	strive
teeth [tiːθ]	teethe [tiːð] 'acquire teeth'
use [juːs]	use [juːz]
wreath [riːθ]	wreathe [riːð]

The words above are mainly basic English words. There are some others which are loan words, which show a parallel distinction.

abuse [əˈbjuːs]	abuse [əˈbjuːz]
advice	advise
device	devise
excuse [eksˈkjuːs]	excuse [eksˈkjuːz]

In all of the examples cited here, the verb has a voiced fricative, the noun has the corresponding voiceless fricative. A pair like *practice* and *practise*, in British English, shares the same spelling pattern with *advice* and *advise*, but both members of the pair are pronounced [ˈpræktɪs].

There are a few pairs where the same change marks the difference between an adjective and a verb. Again, the verb has the voiced member of the pair.

Adjective	*Verb*
safe	save
loth/loath [ləʊθ]	loathe [ləʊð]

There is also a set of words where the verb has a voiced plosive and the corresponding noun ends in a voiceless sound, but sometimes the voiceless sound is a plosive, and sometimes it is a fricative.

Noun	Verb
ascent	ascend
defence (US: defense)	defend
descent	descend
extent	extend
gilt	gild
intent	intend
offence	offend
portent	portend
pretence (US: pretense)	pretend
suspense	suspend

There are also pairs where voicing does not change, but there is a change between plosive and fricative marking a difference between adjective and noun.

Adjective	Noun
abstinent	abstinence
competent	competence
deterrent	deterrence
different	difference
frequent	frequence (or frequency)
impotent	impotence
inadvertent	inadvertence
innocent	innocence
recurrent	recurrence

There are more words of this kind than are listed here, but new ones cannot be added to the set.

Finally, we find some words which differ in the voicing of the final fricative, but where there is also a change in the stressed vowel. The vowel quality is unpredictable, so these words simply have to be learned.

Noun	Verb
bath [bɑ:θ]	bathe [beɪð]
breath [breθ]	breathe [bri:ð]
choice [tʃɔɪs]	choose [tʃu:z]
cloth [klɒθ]	clothe [kləʊð]
glass [glɑ:s]	glaze [gleɪz]
grass [grɑ:s]	graze [greɪz] 'eat grass'
life [laɪf]	live [lɪv]
loss [lɒs]	lose [lu:z]

> POTENTIAL PROBLEM: Although the examples listed above are related in meaning, there are some instances where forms which look parallel are not obviously related in meaning: *intense* does not seem related to *intend*, for example, nor *content* to *contend*.

There are also some very rare examples with a relationship between different parts of speech: *reverend* (adjective) and *reverence* (noun). The distinction between *price* and *prize* may simply be chance, and not morphological: the two come from the same source.

17.2.3 Related Words with Different Stress

There is a set of some hundred two-syllable words where the verb and the related noun are spelt the same, contain the same consonant sounds, and may contain the same vowel sounds, although often the vowel sounds are different depending on the stress. The noun and the verb have different stress patterns, though. This is a very specific case of the general observation that nouns tend to be stressed nearer the beginning than verbs do. So in a word like *import*, stress on the first syllable gives a noun, while stress on the second syllable gives a verb. With the orthographic form <combat>, when the noun is intended (and there is stress on the first syllable), we get ['kɒmbæt], and when the verb is intended (and the stress is on the second syllable), we get [kəm'bæt]. The changes in vowel quality are aligned with the impossibility of having some vowels in stressed syllables and the preference for reduced vowels in completely unstressed syllables.

The difficulty with this pattern is that it is not predictable. *Import* is a member of the set, *report* is not (verb and noun are both stressed on the second syllable). *Address* has initial stress for the noun in US English, but not in British English, where verb and noun are both stressed on the second syllable. *Control* is stressed on the second syllable for both the noun and the verb, *research* is increasingly pronounced with stress on the first syllable for both noun and verb. Part of this unpredictability is that the set of words which can be distinguished in this way varies from generation to generation: old pairs are lost, new pairs are added. While advanced students need to be aware of this potential way of distinguishing nouns from verbs, they must only use words this way when they know there is such a distinction.

Examples:

Spelling	Noun	Verb
affix	['æfiks]	[ə'fiks]
ally	['ælaɪ]	[ə'laɪ]
discount	['dɪskaʊnt]	[dɪs'kaʊnt]
essay	['eseɪ]	[ə'seɪ]
extract	['ekstrækt]	[ɪk'strækt]

Spelling	Noun	Verb
insert	['ɪnsɜːt]	[ɪn'sɜːt]
proceed	['prəʊsiːd]	[prə'siːd]
progress	['prəʊgres] (US: ['prɑːgrəs])	[prə'gres]
prospect	['prɒspekt]	[prə'spekt]
record	['rekəd]	[rɪ'kɔːd]
segment	['segmənt]	[sɪg'ment]
surmise	['sɜːmaɪz]	[sə'maɪz]

Although this pattern usually shows a distinction between noun and verb, in the case of *absent* and *frequent* the adjective is stressed on the first syllable and the verb is stressed on the second.

A rather more complex pattern is found with a much smaller number of words of three or more syllables. Here the main stress stays the same, but the syllables after the main stress get different stress patterns (and may have different vowels). This pattern is particularly found with words spelt with <ment> or <ate> at the end. Here adjectives and nouns behave the same way, differently from verbs. The verbs have secondary stress on the final syllable.

Examples:

Spelling	Noun or Adjective	Verb
appropriate	[ə'prəʊpriət] (A)	[ə'prəʊprieɪt]
compliment	['kɒmplɪmənt] (N)	['kɒmplɪment]
confederate	[kən'fedərət] (A, N)	[kən'fedəreɪt]
elaborate	[ɪ'læbərət] (A)	[ɪ'læbəreɪt]
estimate	['estɪmət] (N)	['estɪmeɪt]
graduate	['grædjʊɪt] (N)	['grædjʊeɪt]
prophesy	['prɒfəsi] (N)	['prɒfəsaɪ]
supplement	['sʌplɪmənt] (N)	['sʌplɪment]

18

LEARNED WORD-FORMATION

A large amount of the English vocabulary is derived, directly or indirectly, from Latin and Greek. Because many of the combinations of elements from these languages are some 2,000 years old or more, the meanings of the combinations are not always predictable, even if you understand the individual elements themselves. This means that even people who understand Latin or Greek may not always be able to work out the precise meanings of the English words derived from these languages. Nevertheless, some understanding of the patterns can provide a useful mnemonic to the meanings of these words in English, and can make their structure less obscure. In this chapter, only a brief introduction can be given to the kinds of structure that can be found in such words, but most native speakers of English have only a hazy idea about these structures, so that any degree of understanding can provide some advantage. On the other hand, this material is only relevant at the very highest level of achievement.

In this chapter just two patterns will be explored: compounds derived from Greek elements and prefixed verbs from Latin.

18.1 Greek Compounds

The compounds that are to be dealt with here are called 'neo-classical' compounds in the literature. Although there are some compounds which follow a Latin pattern, only those which are derived from Greek will be considered here. These compounds provide words which are very technical and scientific, though a few of them (such as *photograph* and *telephone*) have become part of the everyday vocabulary of English.

To illustrate how these compounds work, a few illustrations will be given. The first of these is words ending in *phobia*. *Phobia* is a word on its own in English, meaning 'fear or hatred, especially an extreme or irrational one', but it comes from the Greek word meaning 'fear' with a suffix *-ia*, here meaning 'a pathological condition'. The suffix can be replaced with the suffix *-ic* to provide the corresponding adjective, *phobic*. When there is no suffix, which occurs only in compounds, the compound means 'a person who suffers from the fear'. In the first position in the compound, we find elements which indicate what the person might be afraid of. Because *phobia* begins with a consonant sound, the first elements, where they are Greek, will usually end in *-o*. A good example is *xenophobia*. The element *xeno-* comes from a Greek word meaning 'strange, foreign', and *xenophobia* is a fear (or irrational hatred) of foreigners. The corresponding adjective is *xenophobic*, and the noun for the person who is afraid is *xenophobe*. The element *xeno-* can be found in other words such as *xenogamy*, a biological terms for 'cross-fertilization' (the *gam-* element is literally 'marriage'), or *xenolith*, a geological term for a piece of foreign rock found in magma (the *lith* element means 'stone'). The element *xen-* can also be found in the word *xenon* 'a gas', and can be added to English words, as in *xeno-transplant* 'transplant from a different species'. Since there are irrational fears of many things, so there can be many first elements in such compounds. *Gynephobia* is fear of women (the element *gyne* 'woman' ends in a vowel sound, and so no *-o-* is necessary), *zoophobia* 'fear of animals' (*zo-* means 'animal'), *acrophobia* 'fear of heights' (*acr-* means 'point or summit' and is found also in *acropolis* 'city on a peak'), *pyrophobia* 'fear of fire' (*pyr-* means 'fire') and so on. Sometimes slightly joking terms are created on the pattern, such as *tridecaphobia*, sometimes *triskaidekaphobia*, 'fear of the number 13'. Sometimes first elements are created from English words, as in *Anglophobia* 'fear of the English'. Note that we would expect *hydrophobia*, on this pattern, to mean 'fear of water' (*hydr-* means 'water'), but *hydrophobia* refers to the inability to swallow which is a symptom of rabies, and hence means 'rabies'. The corresponding adjective *hydrophobic* can mean 'relating to rabies', but can also mean 'repelling water' in biological systems. This example shows how words can develop in meaning beyond what can be deduced from their structure. The same phenomenon is, of course, found in English words, too.

As a second example, we will consider the element *hydro-*. We have seen in *hydrophobia* how this works to build up compounds, and there are many similar examples: *hydrogen* 'a gas' (*gen* means 'produce'), *hydrology* 'the study of the use of water resources' (*-ology* usually means 'the study of' and comes from *log-* meaning 'word'), *hydrometry* 'measurement of water' (*metr-* means 'measure'), *hydropathy* 'the treatment of disease by water' (*path-* means 'suffering') and so on. Note *hydraemia* (or US *hydremia*) 'watery blood' (*(h)aem-* means 'blood'), where the second element begins with a vowel sound, and no *-o-* is necessary. The element *hydr-* can also have suffixes attached to it: *hydrate* 'to combine with or absorb water', *hydric* 'to do with an abundance of moisture'. Often *hydro-* is used as a prefix on an ordinary word: *hydrocellulose*, *hydrodynamic*, *hydrosphere* and so on. Sometimes, in the language of chemistry, *hydro-* means 'hydrogen' rather than 'water': *hydrocarbon*, *hydrocortisone*.

As a third example, we will consider the element *phil*, from the Greek word meaning 'love'. We find this in first elements, such as *philanthropy* ('love' + 'human being' + suffix), *philology* ('love' + 'word' + suffix, now meaning 'the study of the history of language'), *philosopher* ('love' + 'wisdom' + suffix), and we can find *phil* used in second elements, with various suffixes, in *bibliophile* ('book' + 'love'; this means 'book-lover' with no suffix for the agent – the addition of the final <e> is found elsewhere, but is not completely regular), *haemophilia* (US *hemophilia*) ('blood' + 'love' + suffix; 'a hereditary disease causing excessive bleeding' – the link with liking or love is obscure), *thermophilic* ('heat' + 'love' + suffix; 'thriving in high temperatures' – used of plants, bacteria, etc.).

Some of the more common elements that recur in such words are provided in the examples below. Remember that some of these may be used as prefixes or suffixes on ordinary English words as well as in neo-classical compounds, and that usually they occur with a final -*o* unless they already end with a vowel sound. Also recall that some of the number prefixes can be used with these bases (see Section 16.4).

Element	Meaning	Example word	Comment
(o)nym	'name'	synonym 'word which means the same as another'; patronymic 'name inherited from one's father'	
bi	'life'	biography 'writing about someone's life'	
cardi	'heart'	tachycardia 'rapid heart beat'	
chron	'time'	anachronism 'something assigned to an incorrect time period'	
crypt	'hidden'	cryptography 'writing in code'	
dem	'people'	democracy 'rule by the people'	
ge	'earth'	geography 'writing about the earth'	
graph	'writing'	photograph 'picture produced by light'	
heli	'sun'	heliocentric 'having the sun as its centre'	
mis	'hatred'	misogyny 'hatred of women'	
neur	'nerve'	neuralgia 'pain in the nerves'; neurolinguistics 'the study of the way language works in the brain'	neur is also used for things connected with the brain
opt	'eye'	myopia 'short sightedness'	

Element	Meaning	Example word	Comment
phon	'sound'	phonology 'the study of the sound systems of language'; Anglophone 'person who speaks English'	
psych	'soul, mind'	psychology 'study of the mind'	
rrh	'flow'	haemorrhage 'bleeding'	
the	'god'	theocracy 'government by the rule of god'	
tom, tm	'cut'	dichotomy 'division into two parts'	

18.2 Latin Verbs

There are many verbs derived from Latin in English where there is, in Latin, a prefix and a base. It is dubious whether these Latin prefixes should count as prefixes in English, largely because their meaning is not fixed, and the interpretation of both prefix and base is so often figurative in some way. Occasionally, however, the Latin structure can give a clue as to the meaning in English, or act as a mnemonic.

The Latin prefixes involved include those listed below, many of which will be familiar from the English prefixes in Chapter 16.

ab–	'from'
ad– (with many different variants)	'to'
ante–	'previous, preceding'
circum–	'around'
co–, con–, com–	'together'
contra–	'against, opposite'
de–	'down'
e–, ex–	'out of'
in–	'in, into'
inter–	'between'
ob–	'opposite'
per–	'through'
peri–	'around, nearby'
pre–	'before'
pro–	'in front of'
re–	'again, back'
trans–	'across'

These Latin prefixes are added to Latin bases, meaningful in Latin, but often not in English. Some of the bases and the combinations they enter into are given below.

Latin base	Latin meaning	Combinations	Comments
ced, ceed, sede	'go, let go'	accede (from ad), antecede, concede, exceed, intercede, precede, proceed, recede	Some of these verbs have nominalizations in -cession
ceive	'take'	conceive, deceive, perceive, receive	All the verbs have nominalizations in -ception
cite	'call'	excite, incite, recite	
clude	'close'	conclude, include, preclude	All the verbs have nominalizations in -clusion
cur	'run'	concur, incur, recur	
dict	'say'	contradict, interdict, predict	All the verbs have nominalizations in -diction. Note indict [ɪnˈdaɪt], with the nominalization indictment, which is not directly from Latin.
duce	'lead'	adduce, conduce, deduce, induce, produce, reduce, transduce	All the verbs have nominalizations in -duction
fend	'strike'	defend, offend (from ob)	
fer	'carry'	confer, defer, infer, prefer, refer	
flect	bend	deflect, inflect, reflect	
ject	'throw'	eject, inject, interject, object, project, reject	All the verbs have nominalizations in -jection
mand	'order'	command, demand, remand	
mit	'put'	admit, commit, emit, permit, remit, transmit	All the verbs have nominalizations in -ission
pel	'push'	compel, expel, impel, propel, repel	All the verbs have nominalizations in -pulsion

Latin base	Latin meaning	Combinations	Comments
plore	'search'	deplore, explore, implore	
port	'carry'	deport, export, report, transport	
rupt	'burst'	erupt, interrupt	All the verbs have nominalizations in *-ruption*
spect	'look'	inspect, expect, prospect, respect	
spire	'breathe'	aspire (from ad), conspire, expire, inspire, perspire, respire, transpire	
tend	'stretch'	attend (from ad), contend, extend, intend, pretend	All the verbs have nominalizations in *-tension*
vade	'go'	evade, invade, pervade	All the verbs have nominalizations in *-vasion*
vene	'come'	convene, contravene, intervene	All the verbs have nominalizations in *-vention*

Note that further generalizations are possible on the basis of these verbs. Many of them, for instance, have adjectives in *-ive*, often with the *-ive* replacing the *-ion* in the nominalization. Sometimes there are words of other word-classes which appear to follow the same patterns: *aspect* is a noun, for example. Such instances have been omitted in the table above.

19

MORPHOLOGY AND FREQUENCY

Frequency lists of English usually provide lemmatized data, which means that we cannot see the relative frequencies of, say, the third person singular, the past tense and the past participle of individual verbs. We can, however, make some assumptions. For example, we can assume that the relative frequencies of the parts of the verb (or of the singular and plural forms of nouns) will depend to some extent on the individual verb or noun concerned. *Died* is likely to be more frequent than *dies*. *Ants* and *children* are likely to be more frequent than *ant* and *child*. But *eagle* is probably more frequent than *eagles*, and *knows* might be more frequent than *knowing*. At the level of the individual words, this is relatively easily checked in large corpora. (All of these are confirmed in COCA.) At the systemic level, it is not clear that it matters much. Because one of the things that we can be fairly sure of is that the individual inflectional affixes are more common than individual derivational affixes. They are all learnt early by children acquiring English as a first language, while some derivational affixes are never learnt by some children (we have recently come across native undergraduates who are apparently unaware of the suffix *-(ia)na* in *Victoriana*). This makes a first decision on teaching morphology relatively easy: inflectional morphology needs to be taught and learnt before derivational morphology. The obligatoriness of inflectional morphology and its automaticity make this highly desirable, and mostly achievable in the regular cases, because it can be done by rule. The only difficulty with such a statement is that it assumes that inflection is relatively homogeneous. That is a false assumption: it is not clear that superlative marking on adjectives, for example, is more regular or more useful than adverbial marking on adjectives, which is usually (but not universally) considered to be a matter of derivation.

When we come to derivational morphology, things become more difficult. We have two measures of usefulness. The first is frequency. How frequently are students likely to be exposed to particular derivational patterns? The second is productivity. To what extent can students trust derivational patterns to allow them to create words when they meet a gap in their active vocabularies? The two do not agree, especially not for students with small vocabularies.

Given that derivation is often defined as having unpredictable gaps in the paradigms it produces (*love* and *hatred* belong to different paradigms, there is a standard word *hateful* but no standard word *loveful*), it might appear that no derivational paradigm would be worth teaching as such. We are of the opinion that such a view is too pessimistic. There are many affixes which are productive enough to allow students to use them in extremis. Some of these are the following:

The use of *-er* on transitive verbs to create agent nouns.
The use of *-able* on transitive verbs to provide adjectives with a modal reading.
The use of *-ation* on verbs ending in *-ize* or *-ify* to create a nominalization.
The use of *-ly* on less frequent adjectives to create adverbs.
The use of *-ish* on adjectives to produce adjectives of approximation.
The use of *-like* on nouns to provide adjectives of similarity.
The use of *un-* on adjectives to provide negatives.
The use of *-ness* on adjectives to make nouns.

The use of such morphology may not always provide the standard English way of expressing the appropriate meaning, nor will it always provide the only way of expressing a particular notion, but it should always provide a comprehensible word in the context. Of course, there are many notions that remain inexpressible by these few processes, but we take the view that having a few reliable arms with which to fight the battle against a strange vocabulary is preferable to having none at all. The less reliable morphology may be used passively to help understand unknown words, but cannot be used to create solutions to problems of expression. Even this is a useful skill to have.

It might seem that in an ideal world, greater productivity would be the result of greater frequency: the more you see a particular construction, the more you can use it. While there is some truth to that, the problem is that it is a question of constructions. Productivity is about new uses of constructions – expanding the number of lexemes in which the construction occurs – while frequency is about established vocabulary which is used all the time because it is known to large numbers of people. Familiar vocabulary often contains constructions which are so old that they have no room for expansion.

A survey of the most common words in the Corpus of Contemporary American English makes it clear that most of the words in the first couple of thousand words are morphologically simple. They simply have to be learnt. But among those words which are morphologically complex, the most frequent nominalization suffix is *-ion* (with its variants, including *-ation*). This is not a reliably productive suffix. The only place where it is reliable, is when added to *-ize* or to

-*ify*. There is only one such word in the first two thousand words of English (*organization*). Similarly, the most frequent adjectival suffix is -*al*. This is not a reliable way of forming adjectives in current English at all. The suffix -*ish*, which is more reliable, does not appear until the second thousand words, where there are two types. But they are not the reliable pattern, they are in words denoting nationality/ethnicity: *English* and *Jewish*. It is not until the third thousand words that -*er*, a reliable suffix, starts to overtake -*ment*, an unreliable suffix, in the formation of nouns (though clearly with different meanings). The only place where frequency and productivity seem to align is with adverbial -*ly*, which is common, and the most common way of forming adverbs, from the earliest stages, and is so productive that some authorities consider it to be inflectional.

The clear conclusion is that students cannot be left to deduce productivity based on the frequency of morphological constructions in the words they know. To deduce productivity you have to be sensitive to frequency in words you do not know, and second language learners have vocabularies which are too small for this to be a viable strategy. The implication is that students need to be taught what is productive and what is not. In this book we have tried to distinguish between what can be used actively and what can only be used passively for analysis. Both can be useful, but they play different roles in the learning process.

READING AND SOURCES

For derivational morphology, in particular, our reliance on Bauer et al. (2013) will be very obvious, although we do not always use the same terminology. For inflectional morphology we have used not only Bauer et al. (2013), but also the two major reference grammars of English, Quirk et al. (1985) and Huddleston and Pullum (2002), which we also recommend for the uses of the various inflected forms. Bauer et al. (2013) frequently cite other sources, which we have thus used indirectly. On classical elements in English word-formation, we have referred to Stockwell and Minkova (2001). The Corpus of Contemporary American English (COCA) can be found at Davies (2008).

For introductory material on morphological theory, we recommend Bauer (2003) and Lieber (2010) among the many such introductions. We have used several dictionaries, most notably the *Oxford English dictionary* (OED) online and *The Chambers dictionary* (Brookes 2006). We have also referred to a number of dictionaries of English pronunciation.

Bauer, L. 2003. *Introducing linguistic morphology*. Edinburgh: Edinburgh University Press.

Bauer, L., R. Lieber & I. Plag. 2013. *The Oxford reference guide to English morphology*. Oxford: Oxford University Press.

Brookes, I. (ed.) 2006. *The Chambers dictionary*. Edinburgh: Chambers Harrap.

Davies, M. 2008. *The corpus of contemporary American English (COCA)*. www.americancorpus.org

Huddleston, R. & G. K. Pullum (eds) 2002. *The Cambridge grammar of the English language*. Cambridge: Cambridge University Press.

Lieber, R. 2010. *Introducing morphology*. Cambridge: Cambridge University Press.

OED. *The Oxford English dictionary* online. www.oed.com

Quirk, R., S. Greenbaum, G. Leech & J. Svartvik. 1985. *A comprehensive grammar of the English language*. Harlow: Longman.

Stockwell, R. & D. Minkova. 2001. *English words*. Cambridge: Cambridge University Press.

INDEX OF AFFIXES AND OTHER BOUND ELEMENTS

INDEX OF SUBJECTS

Note: **Bold** text indicates particularly important coverage.

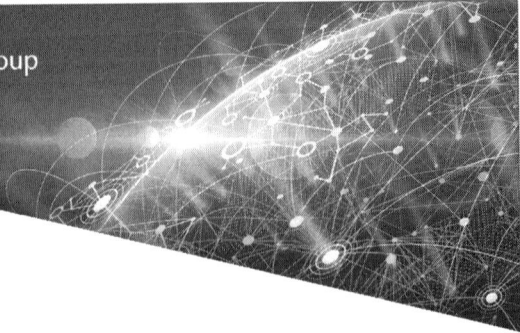